Lafayette

The World Generals Series

"Palgrave's World Generals Series features great leaders whose reputations have transcended their own nations, whose bold characters led to new forms of combat, whose determination and courage gave shape to new dynasties and civilizations—men whose creativity and courage inspired multitudes. Beginning with illustrious World War II German Field Marshal Irwin Rommel, known as the Desert Fox, the series sheds new light on famous warrior-leaders such as Napoleon, Frederick the Great, Alexander, Julius Caesar, and Genghis Khan, drawing out the many important leadership lessons that are still relevant to our lives today."

—*General Wesley K. Clark (Ret.)*

This distinguished new series features the lives of eminent military leaders from around the world who changed history. Top military historians are writing concise but comprehensive biographies including the personal lives, battles, strategies, and legacies of these great generals, with the aim to provide background and insight into contemporary armies and wars, as well as to draw lessons for the leaders of today.

Rommel by Charles Messenger

Alexander the Great by Bill Yenne

Montgomery by Trevor Royle

Lafayette by Marc Leepson

Ataturk by Austin Bay

De Gaulle by Michael Haskew

Giap by James Warren

Julius Caesar by Bill Yenne

Lafayette

Lessons in Leadership from the Idealist General

Marc Leepson

palgrave
macmillan

for Dee

LAFAYETTE
Copyright © Marc Leepson, 2011.

First published in 2011 by
PALGRAVE MACMILLAN®
in the United States—a division of St. Martin's Press LLC,
175 Fifth Avenue, New York, NY 10010.

Where this book is distributed in the UK, Europe and the rest of the world,
this is by Palgrave Macmillan, a division of Macmillan Publishers Limited,
registered in England, company number 785998, of Houndmills, Basingstoke,
Hampshire RG21 6XS.

Palgrave Macmillan is the global academic imprint of the above companies and
has companies and representatives throughout the world.

Palgrave® and Macmillan® are registered trademarks in the United States, the
United Kingdom, Europe and other countries.

ISBN: 978–0–230–10504–1

Library of Congress Cataloging-in-Publication Data

Leepson, Marc, 1945–
    Lafayette : lessons in leadership from the idealist general / Marc Leepson ;
foreword by General Wesley K. Clark.
        p. cm.
    ISBN 978–0–230–10504–1
    1. Lafayette, Marie Joseph Paul Yves Roch Gilbert Du Motier, marquis
de, 1757–1834—Military leadership. 2. United States—History—
Revolution, 1775–1783—Participation, French. 3. France—History—
Revolution, 1789–1799. 4. France—History—Consulate and First Empire,
1799–1815. 5. France—History—July Revolution, 1830. 6. Generals—
France—Biography. 7. Generals—United States—Biography.
8. Statesmen—France—Biography. 9. France. Armée—Biography.
10. Command of troops—Case studies. I. Title.

DC146.L2L44 2011
355.0092—dc22   2010030359

A catalogue record of the book is available from the British Library.

Design by Newgen Imaging Systems (P) Ltd., Chennai, India.

First edition: March 2011

10 9 8 7 6 5 4 3 2 1

Printed in the United States of America.

Contents

Eight pages of black and white illustrations
appear between pages 98 and 99.

Acknowledgments

THIS BOOK RESULTED FROM A CONVERSATION THAT MY FRIEND AND
literary agent, Joseph Brendan Vallely, had with Alessandra Bastagli,
the editor of the *Great Generals* series at Palgrave Macmillan. Many
thanks to Joe and to Alessandra and her staff, including assistant editor Colleen Lawrie, in New York, as well as associate production editor Erica Warren and copyeditor Jay Harward, and to General Wesley
Clark, the series editor.

Thanks, too, to Diane Windham Shaw, the special collections
librarian and college archivist at Lafayette College in Pennsylvania,
who provided invaluable research advice from the very beginning of
this project, as well as many of the images. And to Ellen McCallister
Clark, the library director at the Society of the Cincinnati in
Washington D.C., and Elizabeth Frengel, manager of reader services, for their much-needed help with images, among other research
materials.

I want to thank my friend Susan Stein, the Gilder curator and vice
president for museum programs at the Thomas Jefferson Foundation
at Monticello, for her support and guidance. Thanks, too, to the ter-
rific folks at the Middleburg Library in Loudoun County, Virginia,
especially Branch Manager Sheila Whetzel. And to my friends at the

Library of Virginia in Richmond, especially Tom Camden, director of special collections; Audrey Johnson, senior rare book librarian; Minor Weisiger, archives research services; and Sandy Treadway, the Librarian of Virginia.

Special thanks to MaryBeth McIntire, executive director of the Library of Virginia Foundation; Elise Geffel and Dan Stackhouse at the LOVF; and to my colleagues on the LOVF Board and the Library of Virginia Board of Trustees. Thanks to my colleagues at Vietnam Veterans America national headquarters, especially my great editor and good friend Michael Keating.

I've been fortunate to have had support and encouragement from many friends and family members: Xande Anderer, Cliff Boyle, Bernie and Linda Brien, Amoret Bruguiere, Childs Burden, Bob Carolla, Shane Chalke, Dave Condon, Larry Cushman, John Czaplewski, Diane Deitz, Gayle and Tom DeLashmutt, Laurie DeMaris, Benton Downer, Patrick Sheane Duncan, Dale Dye, Bill and Sue Ferster, Fred Geary, Rob Gwynn, John and Donna Hoffecker, Wayne Karlin, Dean King, Evan Leepson, Peter and Ellen Leepson, Margaret Littleton, Treavor Lord, and Hunt Lyman.

And: Greg McNamee, Dave Miller, Mike Morency, Josh Muss, Katherine Neville, Margaret New, Tom and Ann Northrup, Angus Paul, Mike Powers, Karl Pribram, Susan Price, Dan and Margie Radovsky, Moses Robbins, Peter Schwartz, Margo Sherman, Peggy Stalnaker, Susan and Fraser Wallace, David and Michele Willson, Bob and Martha Wilson, and Susan and Saul Zucker.

Special thanks to my wife, Janna, for putting up with my too-long, seven-day-a-week writing schedule; to my children, Cara and Devin, for their support; and to my dear Aunt Sally Sherman, who I miss every day.

And to Google Books: you have saved me countless hours, days, and months of research time. Keep digitizing.

Foreword

ALMOST EVERY SCHOOLCHILD LEARNS THAT A YOUNG FRENCHMAN named Lafayette came to America during the Revolutionary War and helped George Washington. Some may recall that afterward he returned to France. But Lafayette's remarkable lifetime of contributions to two nations may be unique in military history. Marc Leepson's compelling biography brings to life this extraordinary story of courage, contradictions, and lasting contributions.

At the age of nineteen, young Lafayette, a French nobleman whose father died fighting the English, defies his king, escapes France, and arrives in the rebelling colonies. There he seeks out General George Washington, presses for a commission in the American Army, leads troops in battle, and becomes a successful American general. He later returns to France and plays a pivotal role time and again in transitioning his country from a monarchy to a democratic form of government. It could be the stuff of fiction, a fanciful eighteenth-century tale of romance and adventure. But the bare facts make an even better story.

Lafayette was brought up in wealth, and married at sixteen into one of the most privileged families of the French nobility. He had been schooled from childhood for a warrior's role. He was passionate in his military ardor, and unashamed to proclaim his own pursuit of glory at enormous personal sacrifice and risk. By 1776, at the age of eighteen, he had determined that he would find a way to join the American cause so he could fight against the British and for the principles of liberty. He met with American representatives in Paris to plot his destiny and risked his reputation and future by sneaking out of France and going to fight in America against the orders of the king.

In America, he proved himself an able and energetic battlefield commander. He was an ingenious and clever planner, courageous under fire. He adroitly sidestepped early mistakes and came to display incredible judgment and maturity in battlefield command. He was given a division to command, and he proved himself again and again as one of Washington's best and most resourceful commanders. He was a real general—even by the age of twenty.

Lafayette wasn't afraid of his wealth and privilege. He used it, proving his commitment to the cause, earning loyalty from his men, and strengthening the Colonies' ability to wage war. Perhaps it was the fact of his French noble upbringing that helped gain him the respect of his American soldiers. On more than one occasion, he bought equipment, clothing, and provisions for American troops under his command. He also politicked hard with the Continental Congress and American governors and officials to support the army effort. His youth, while startling today, was a little less unusual then and proved no impediment.

In the process, he formed an unbreakable personal bond of trust, friendship, and mutual respect with General George Washington himself. It was an intensely personal relationship. Washington both respected Lafayette's military talents and trusted his motives. This bond, in turn, forged the strategic relationship with France that turned the tide of war and ultimately spelled Britain's defeat.

Lafayette used his position and experiences with the Americans to lobby forcefully for active and continuing French support and participation in the war against England. He mounted letter-writing campaigns. He also returned home to argue the case in person, and indeed, without his voice, the crucial French-American relationship might never have formed. Thus, he displayed a rare talent for the strategic and political levels of war.

Lafayette also was an integral part of the climactic battle at Yorktown, commanding a large element of the American forces, liaising with the French, and adding his persuasive voice to planning. He was only twenty-four at the time.

In America, his achievements were substantial, colorful, and well reported. He deservedly became a real hero here, and remains so today. When he returned to France, the young general returned as a hero there also.

Then, a few years later, as France descended into revolutionary chaos, Lafayette emerged again. He became a political leader in the newly formed National Assembly and authored one of the most influential and famous political tracts in history, the Declaration of the Rights of Man. Then he answered the call of duty to create and form a French National Guard to maintain order. As its commander, he attempted to mediate between radicals and noblemen, and for more than a year maintained his precarious balance between a revolutionary rabble and an intemperate royalty, and helped move France away from an absolute monarchy and into a more liberal form of government. On several occasions he saved the lives of the royal family, and tamped down the worst outbreaks of hateful violence.

Ultimately, though, the middle ground was impossible to maintain. Lafayette and his immediate family were lucky to escape with their lives. After years in exile and imprisonment abroad, he was permitted to return to France, refused service under Napoleon, and then in the twilight of Bonaparte's empire emerged to denounce him, help restore the French monarchy, and finally, years later, push the monarchy into a more moderate, constitutionally restrained form.

Lafayette always seemed to have an instinct for being present at the decisive point. It served him and our country in good stead during the American Revolution. But unlike most military men, he was largely able to employ the same strategic skill in politics. On three occasions over a span of a half century Lafayette was there, at the crucial moment, to shape the emergence of democracy and liberal government. No military leader has done more.

It is no wonder, then, that so many cities, towns, and counties in America carry his name. When in 1917 the American forces under General Pershing arrived in France, there were cries of "Lafayette, we are here." Our first wartime air element bore his name as the "Lafayette Escadrille." He not only bridged two nations, he helped form them. Even today, our army is organized along the lines of the staff model we learned from our French allies in World War II. And Lafayette's legacy serves still to maintain a crucial relationship between two armies, and two democracies.

—General Wesley K. Clark (Ret.)

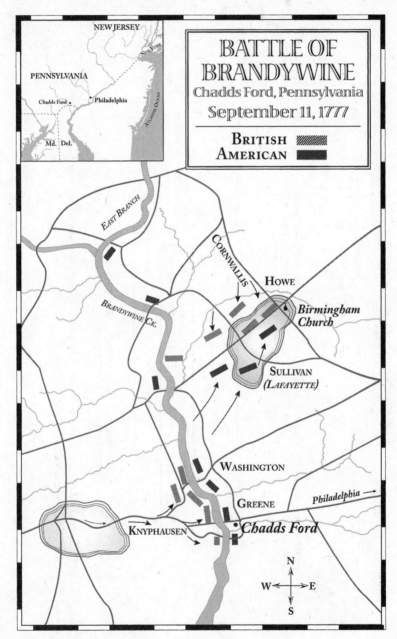

Map of the Battle of Brandywine. Credit: Liz Weaver

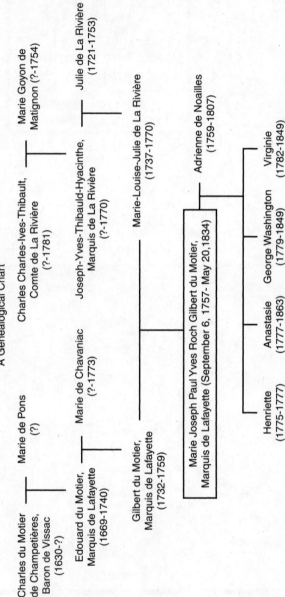

Gilbert du Motier, the Marquis de Lafayette
A Genealogical Chart

Charles du Motier
de Champetières,
Baron de Vissac
(1630-?)

Marie de Pons
(?)

Charles Charles-Ives-Thibault,
Comte de La Rivière
(?-1781)

Marie Goyon de
Matignon (?-1754)

Edouard du Motier,
Marquis de Lafayette
(1669-1740)

Marie de Chavaniac
(?-1773)

Joseph-Yves-Thibauld-Hyacinthe,
Marquis de La Rivière
(?-1770)

Julie de La Rivière
(1721-1753)

Gilbert du Motier,
Marquis de Lafayette
(1732-1759)

Marie-Louise-Julie de La Rivière
(1737-1770)

Marie Joseph Paul Yves Roch Gilbert du Motier,
Marquis de Lafayette (September 6, 1757- May 20,1834)

Adrienne de Noailles
(1759-1807)

Henriette
(1775-1777)

Anastasie
(1777-1863)

George Washington
(1779-1849)

Virginie
(1782-1849)

Source: Stanley J. Idzerda, et al., eds., *Lafayette in the Age of the American Revolution: Selected Letters and Papers, 1776-1790*
(Ithaca, New York: Cornell University Press, 1980), Vol. III

An Essential Friend to America

The moment I heard of America, I loved her; the moment I knew she was fighting for freedom, I burnt with a desire of bleeding for her.

—Marquis de Lafayette, 1778[1]

We cherish his memory above that of any citizen of a foreign country.

—President Franklin D. Roosevelt, May 20, 1934[2]

IN THE SPRING OF 1778, IN THE FOURTH YEAR OF THE AMERICAN REVOLUTION, the government of France signed a treaty with the United States, joining the American war of independence against Great Britain.

The British reacted to this portentous development by declaring war against France and by moving 5,000 troops from North America to the Caribbean and all of their troops from Philadelphia to New York City and Rhode Island.

When word reached General George Washington's camp in Valley Forge in mid-May that the British appeared to be starting to evacuate Philadelphia, the American commander in chief sent his twenty-year-old French volunteer major general, the Marquis de Lafayette, with a force of some 2,200 men toward the city.

"You will remember that your detachment is a very valuable one, and that any accident happening to it would be a severe blow to this Army," Washington said in his May 18 order to Lafayette, who had had his baptism by fire at the Battle of Brandywine eight months earlier. "You will therefore use every possible precaution for its security, and to guard against a surprise."[3]

It turned out that there was a surprise. When British general William Howe in Philadelphia learned on May 19 that Lafayette was heading toward the city, Howe vowed that he would capture the precocious Frenchman. At 10:30 P.M., Howe moved some 5,000 troops with fourteen cannons under General James Grant out of Philadelphia to circle behind Lafayette. Howe then led the rest of his army, about 6,000 men, to face Lafayette head-on.

The next morning, May 20, Lafayette arrived at Barren Hill (known today as Lafayette Hill) in far northwest Philadelphia, near the Chestnut Hill neighborhood, where a most unpleasant surprise awaited: he found himself in a dangerously exposed position nearly surrounded by Grant and Howe's troops.

"It was in the presence of the troops that he first heard the cry that he was surrounded," Lafayette later wrote in the third person, "and he was forced to smile at the unpleasant intelligence."[4]

Cool under pressure, Lafayette quickly realized the dire situation he faced. Always aggressive, he took two immediate steps that staved off disaster. First, he faked an all-out attack using about 500 men, including some 50 Oneida Indians led by Captain Allan McLane, a Philadelphia native. Grant took the bait and ordered his men to halt and form a line of battle.

While they did, Lafayette calmly ordered a company-by-company orderly retreat down the steep slope of the hill behind him to a hidden road along the Schuylkill River. He then led all of his troops, including McLane and his men, back across the Schuylkill, and they quick-marched safely back to Valley Forge. The British didn't realize that Lafayette had orchestrated a miraculous escape until they finally charged what they thought was Lafayette's camp from two directions and found it deserted.

General Howe, furious at Lafayette's escape, ordered his men to march back to Philadelphia; he reportedly refused to speak to Grant as they trudged back to the former American capital. Howe, following his usual nonaggressive pattern, did not order any kind of counterattack. The next day, May 21, he sailed for England, and General Henry Clinton took over the forces of King George III in the United States.

❖

That small engagement demonstrates the hallmarks of Lafayette's long and impressive military career. He exhibited his best traits that day at Barren Hill: confidence, courage, and aggressiveness. But he also acted impetuously, disregarding Washington's order to be cautious and avoid being surprised by the British. Still, Lafayette learned an important lesson from that youthful experience. He went on to curb his impetuousness (for the most part) and controlled his aggressiveness during the Revolution. Lafayette proved to be one of the most important military—and political—players in that war, as well as in the French Revolution, which began in 1789, and the French July Revolution of 1830.

✦

This concise biography of Lafayette looks primarily at his life and times on the field of battle. During the American Revolution and the two French revolutions, he faced physical hardship, mental anguish, the threat of imminent death, and the frustrations of military bureaucracy. But Lafayette never wavered from his dedication to the ideals of individual freedom and republican—versus unfettered monarchical—government. He proved time and again that he was willing to put his life on the line in pursuit of his beliefs.

As Lafayette put it in a letter to Thomas Jefferson in the spring of 1781, six months before the British surrender at Yorktown: "My respects for the rights and conveniences of the citizens cannot be equaled but by my zeal to forward every means of securing their freedom."[5]

CHAPTER 1

An Ancient Family of Warriors

From the time I was eight, I longed for glory.

—Marquis de Lafayette[1]

MARIE JOSEPH PAUL YVES ROCH GILBERT DU MOTIER DE LA FAYETTE,
the man we know as the Marquis de Lafayette, was born on September
6, 1757. He came into this world in an ornate bedchamber on the top
floor of his family's eighteen-room, two-towered, fourteenth-century
Normanesque stone castle known as the Chateau de Chavaniac.
Surrounded by a moat, formal gardens, and ponds, the imposing
chateau sits outside its namesake small village, Chavaniac-Lafayette,
about 300 miles south of Paris in the mountainous Auvergne region
of south-central France.[2]

Historians have traced Lafayette's venerable paternal line back to about the year 1000. Nearly all of the family's males made their mark fighting in France's wars, from the Crusades to the Seven Years' War, and many of them perished on the field of battle.

One of the most honored of Lafayette's ancestors—one who did not die in battle—was Gilbert Motier de La Fayette. One of Gilbert de La Fayette's notable accomplishments during his long, distinguished military career was leading combined French and Scottish forces in defeating the English on March 21, 1421. The site was the Battle of Baugé, near Angers in Normandy, during the Hundred Years' War. According to family lore, in that pivotal engagement, de La Fayette, whose motto was *Cur non?* ("Why not?"), had a hand in the killing of the first Duke of Clarence, the second son of England's King Henry V.

France's King Charles VI honored Gilbert de La Fayette by naming him Marshal of France (*maréchal de france*) in 1421. He also is remembered for fighting at the side of the iconic French national heroine Joan of Arc at the famed 1428 siege of Orléans.

The Motier de La Fayette family settled in Auvergne in the eleventh century. Lafayette's great-grandfather Charles, another illustrious military man, received the title of marquis for his valor on the battlefield. Charles's son Edouard purchased the Chateau de Chavaniac, which dated from the fourteenth century but had burned to the ground and was rebuilt beginning in the last years of the seventeenth century.

Members of the La Fayette family were among Auvergne's most prominent citizens for generations. However, none of them were well known on the French national stage or at the Versailles court. Edouard's son Gilbert, Lafayette's father, was a colonel in the French grenadiers. He died, along with thousands of other French soldiers, on August 1, 1759, at the Battle of Minden in Westphalia (in northern Germany) during the Seven Years' War. His older brother,

Jacques-Roch, died in a 1733 battle in Austria, leaving the marquis title to the much-younger Gilbert.

Lafayette's mother, Marie-Louise, was a member of the La Rivières, one of the oldest and most influential noble French families.[3] Lafayette's great-grandfather Charles-Ives-Thibault, the Comte de La Rivière, was a highly decorated lieutenant in the French royal army. He received the Grand Cross for exceptional merit of the Royal and Military Order of Saint Louis, the French king's highest military award. Until he retired in 1766, La Rivière was a captain-lieutenant and the commandant of the Black Musketeers, the Second Company of the *Mousquetaires du Roi,* the king's Musketeers. The musketeers were the real-life personal bodyguards of the French kings, immortalized by the French novelist Alexandre Dumas in his famed 1844 story of four swashbuckling young men in the court of King Louis XIII.

◆

When Lafayette's father, Gilbert, married Marie-Louise-Julie de La Rivière, she had an extensive dowry, including properties in Brittany, along with an entrée into royal society in Versailles. Marie Joseph Paul Yves Roch Gilbert du Motier de La Fayette, the couple's first child, was baptized at the small Catholic church near the family chateau. Neither his mother nor his father attended the ceremony. Marie-Louise was still recovering from giving birth; Gilbert was off fighting and, in fact, died before seeing his son.

The death of Lafayette's father at the hands of the British—he was, Lafayette later wrote, "carried off by a ball from an English battery, commanded by a certain General Phillips"—had a strong impact on the young boy.[4] Growing up, his grandmother repeatedly and forcefully reminded him that his father had been killed by the British.

Lafayette lived the life of a pampered, doted-upon noble child at Chavaniac. Following the death of his infant sister in 1760, Lafayette's mother spent long periods of time at the Versailles court and in Paris with her father and grandfather. The young Gilbert stayed home in Chavaniac, where he came under the tutelage of his grandmother and two aunts, and grew up in the company of his cousin Marie de Guèrin, a surrogate younger sister. He was the pampered young male heir—a handsome, red-haired, blue-eyed, fair-skinned boy who ran wild in the forests and along the village's streets, wooden sword in hand, playing war games with the peasant boys of the town.

Gilbert and Marie's tutor, Abbé Fayon, spiced up his reading, writing, arithmetic, and language (French and Latin) lessons with tales of the exploits of the Gallic chieftain Vercingetorix, who waged guerrilla war against Caesar's Roman legions in Auvergne. Fayon also recounted stories of the military triumphs of generations of Lafayette men. "It was natural that I grew up hearing many tales of war and glory in the family so closely tied to memories and sorrows associated with war," Lafayette later said.[5] "From the time I was eight," he wrote in his memoirs, "I longed for glory. I remember nothing of my childhood more than my fervor for tales of glory and my plans to travel the world in quest of fame."[6]

The idyllic life ended at Chavaniac in 1768 when Lafayette, not yet twelve years old, submitted to his mother and great-grandfather's will and moved north to Paris. He was to live with them and with his maternal grandfather, the Comte de La Rivière, who was a widower as was Lafayette's great-grandfather. Lafayette's new home was a spacious suite of self-contained luxury apartments given to his great-grandfather by the king in the opulent Palais du Luxembourg on Paris's Left Bank in the Latin Quarter.

It took a week for Lafayette's carriage to reach Paris, where he joined his mother and for the first time met his great-grandfather, his grandfather (Joseph-Yves-Thibauld-Hyacinthe, the Comte de La

Rivière), and uncle (the Comte de Lusignem). The world of the young man who was the center of his small provincial universe abruptly changed. Although his tutor, Abbé Fayon, came with him to Paris, young Gilbert left behind the carefree, lord-of-the-manor existence at Chavaniac and faced life in France's largest city as a naïve, young, pampered boy from the provinces.

It was soon decided that the boy would carry on family tradition and become a military man, something that Lafayette happily accepted. The first step was to enroll him in the Collège du Plessis, an exclusive school for children of the nobility. Faculty from the nearby Sorbonne supervised the teaching at the Collège, where for four years Lafayette studied mathematics, history, geography, French literature, theology, law, and rhetoric. He also read the works of the later Roman Republic's poets and philosophers (including Cicero, Seneca, and Plutarch) and Caesar's *Commentaries,* all in the original Latin.

His Latin studies at the Collège included accounts of Vercingetorix's heroic defense of Lafayette's Auvergne homeland against the Romans in the first century BC, something that cemented the boy's appreciation for the military exploits of his hometown hero. Lafayette later said that he "had a higher regard for Vercingetorix defending our mountains than for Clovis [who first united France] and his successors." He added that he "would much rather have been Vercingetorix defending the mountains of Auvergne."[7]

On April 3, 1770, tragedy struck when, after a brief illness, Lafayette's mother died at age thirty-two at Luxembourg Palace. Just three weeks later, his grief-stricken great-grandfather, the Comte de La Rivière, also died. With those deaths, the thirteen-year-old Lafayette inherited an enormous fortune. Overnight he became one of the richest people in France, inheriting vast lands in Brittany and an income of 120,000 livres a year, roughly equivalent to more than a million of today's American dollars.

Before he died, Lafayette's great-grandfather saw to it that the young boy enrolled in his old royal regiment, the Black Musketeers. And on April 9, 1771, six months before his fourteenth birthday and almost exactly one year after his mother and great-grandfather's deaths, Lafayette was commissioned a *sous-lieutenant* (the lowest officer rank). It was a largely ceremonial job, one that barely took him away from his studies. But the youthful lieutenant did get to take part in Black Musketeer activities such as marching in military reviews and parades and presenting himself in uniform at court in Versailles to King Louis XV.

Through his connections at the court, Lafayette's great-grandfather arranged for the young teenager to marry into another immensely wealthy French family, and one with royal blood, the Noailles. This powerful and influential family was headed by Jean-Paul-François de Noailles, the Duc d'Ayen, who was a brigadier general in the army of King Louis XV.

After months of negotiations (in which the betrothed couple did not take part; Adrienne's father and one of Lafayette's uncles made all the arrangements), the adults signed a marriage contract on February 15, 1773. Because royal blood was involved, Louis XV also signed the contract along with his three sons, all of whom would later become kings of France. The contract included a dowry of 200,000 livres. Lafayette's marriage to Marie Adrienne Francoise de Noailles, known as Adrienne, did not take place until April 11, 1774. He was sixteen; she would turn fifteen six months later. As John Quincy Adams put it in an 1834 speech, a eulogy, Lafayette was joined with "the house of Noailles, the most distinguished family of the Kingdom, scarcely deemed in public consideration inferior to that which wore the Crown."[8]

Abigail Adams, who formed a fast friendship with Adrienne, described her as a warm, unpretentious woman who was devoted to her husband and children. The first time they met, Abigail said, Adrienne "met me at the door, and with the freedom of an old acquaintance, and the rapture peculiar to the ladies of this nation, caught me by the hand and gave me a salute upon each cheek, most heartily rejoiced to see me. You would have supposed I had been some long absent friend, whom she dearly loved."[9]

Within days after the marriage contract was signed in 1773, the adults moved young Lafayette into a suite of rooms in the Noailles family's palatial mansion in Versailles. The family had other residences, including one in Paris; but during the time they spent in Versailles, the betrothed teenagers had the opportunity to get acquainted for the first time. By all indications they fell in love and would remain happily married until her death in 1808.

The move to Versailles also meant the end of Lafayette's days at the Collège du Plessis. The family first arranged for him to take lessons at home again from Abbé Fayon and a former military officer named Margelay. The plan was for the young descendant of warriors to continue on the path to a military career, which included lessons at the riding academy in Versailles. One of Lafayette's fellow students there was another young teenager, the Comte d'Artois, the future King Charles X.

Lafayette's future in-laws then arranged for the boy to attend the prestigious Académie de Versailles. Because one of his wedding gifts from the Duc de Noailles was the promise of commanding a company in his family cavalry regiment upon turning eighteen, Lafayette received a lieutenant's commission in the Noailles Dragoons on April 7, 1773.

The wedding of Gilbert Lafayette and Adrienne Noailles took place in the small chapel at the Noailles mansion in Paris. The reception that followed was a lavish affair that attracted members of the royal family, diplomats, and aristocrats from across the Continent. It included a feast of more than a hundred appetizers, stews, meats, salads, and desserts. After the wedding, the newlyweds moved into a wing of the Noailles Paris mansion.

Soon thereafter, Lafayette took part in summer maneuvers with his regiment at the headquarters of the French Army of the East at Metz, just inside the Prussian border. His two closest fellow officers were his flamboyant brother-in-law, the eighteen-year-old Vicomte de Noailles, and the twenty-one-year-old Louis, Comte de Ségur.

✦

When he returned to Paris in September of 1774, Lafayette reluctantly heeded his in-laws' wishes and plunged into life at the court of twenty-year-old King Louis XVI, who had acceded to the throne in May following the death of Louis XV. Lafayette, his young wife, and her relatives were often in the company of Queen Marie Antoinette and her court. But Lafayette was too taciturn and unsophisticated, and he did not care for the frivolousness of the infamously decadent court life that the queen fashioned at Versailles. Lafayette was not a big drinker, and he was a bad dancer. He simply did not fit in.

Lafayette later spoke of the "unfavorable opinion" that his silence earned him at the French court: "I did not heed and scarcely listened to things that did not appear to be worthy of discussion. That...inclination to be observant was not moderated by the awkwardness of my manners, which...never succumbed to the graces of the court....And when my wife's family obtained a place for me at court, I did not hesitate to be disagreeable to preserve my independence."[10]

Lafayette lived the life of the reluctant courtier and enthusiastic young officer for two more years. He received a promotion to captain in the Noailles Dragoons on May 19, 1775, and continued to serve in that cavalry unit, making periodic trips to French Army headquarters at Metz. Life in the summer garrison was far from spartan. The young officers, Lafayette included, more or less carried on there as they did at court: with plenty of drinking, gambling, and womanizing. Nevertheless, Lafayette and the other officers did learn most of the military basics at Metz, spending time drilling troops and learning tactics and strategy from the experienced (and lower-class) professional officers.

In the summer of 1775, the seventeen-year-old captain had a portentous meeting in Metz with the British Duke of Gloucester, the younger, disaffected brother of King George III. The duke was out of favor in the House of Hanover for marrying the illegitimate daughter of the famed diarist and author Horace Walpole.

In August, the duke and his wife came to Metz, where the Comte Charles-François de Broglie, the French Army commander and innovative military leader who was rabidly anti-British, invited the royal couple to be the guests of honor at a dinner with his officers. The young Marquis de Lafayette, the Vicomte de Noailles, and the Comte de Ségur were among the guests.

Both Broglie and the Duke of Gloucester were Freemasons, and the talk at the table dealt with Masonic ideas of equality and the rights of man. The Frenchmen also received an earful from the English duke about his brother's inadequacies and mistakes, which included waging war against the rebellious American colonists, a conflict that had begun in earnest in April of that year with the Battles of Lexington and Concord.

The atmosphere was decidedly pro-American and anti-British. The latter sentiment had a strong appeal to Lafayette, who had grown up loathing the British for killing his father. Lafayette, along with the other French officers, also believed strongly that if England put down the American colonial rebellion, it would tip the global balance of power and set the British on the road to taking over France's overseas possessions. An American victory over the British, on the other hand, would greatly diminish England's vast international empire.

Lafayette, his brother-in-law, and Ségur left that dinner fired up about the American cause and the tenets of Freemasonry. In Paris, they enthusiastically joined other like-minded young men in intellectual and political clubs where they discussed these and other burning issues of the day. On December 15, 1775, the three young men joined the newly established Saint-Jean de la Candeur Masonic Lodge, one of a dozen "Lodges of Adoption" in the city and one that consisted primarily of members of the nobility.[11]

In March of 1776, the king named the Comte de St. Germain to be the new war minister. St. Germain instituted a series of reforms, including abolishing some regiments and reducing the number of officers from the privileged classes. Among the eliminated companies was the Black Musketeers, Lafayette's former regiment. His current unit, the Noailles Dragoons, was reorganized and a good number of its young, inexperienced, upper-class officers were relegated to part-time duty.

Lafayette was a prime candidate for demotion, with no battle experience and having had his wife's powerful family all but purchase his commission. He was relieved from active duty on June 11, 1776, and made a captain of the reserves less than a month before the rebellious American colonies officially declared their independence from England. The demotion did not exactly bode well for Lafayette's ambition to become a career military officer in the French Army. Nor did the fact that France was not at war, and it did not appear there were any conflicts brewing on the horizon.

Word of the July 4, 1776, Declaration of Independence did not reach France until the fall of that year. When Lafayette learned what happened, he later said, "my heart espoused warmly the cause of liberty, and I thought of nothing but of adding also the aid of my banner."[12] He knew that his wife's family would object, and because he was under twenty-five, Lafayette would need his in-laws' permission to go overseas. His family did not want the young husband leaving France for several reasons, one of them being that his wife had, on December 15, given birth to their first child, Henriette.

But the young man was determined.

"I depended, therefore, solely upon myself," he said, "and I ventured to adopt for a device on my arms these words, '*Cur non?*' that they might equally serve as an encouragement to myself, and as a reply to others."[13]

The Comte de Broglie at first counseled him not to go to America. The count had seen war firsthand; he had, in fact, been with Lafayette's father when he was killed at Minden. "I will not be accessory to the ruin of the only remaining branch of your family," he told Lafayette.[14]

But Lafayette would not be swayed. He was aided in his persistence by his adventurous brother-in-law, the Vicomte de Noailles, and by their close friend, the Comte de Ségur, both of whom also longed to go to America.

Lafayette's stubborn determination overcame Broglie's resistance. Broglie was not acting completely out of a sense of altruism. He had big ambitions of his own—to go to America and take over as commander-in-chief in the fight against the British. Getting one of the richest young French officers in his debt, Broglie knew, could only help his audacious plan.

Months earlier, Broglie had introduced Lafayette to another ardent supporter of the American cause against England, Johan de Kalb. A German-born veteran of the Seven Years' War, Kalb had served under Broglie at the Metz garrison. In 1768, Kalb had ventured to the American colonies on a secret mission for France's Secretary of State Étienne François, the Duke of Choiseul, to assess the military situation there. Nothing came of that assignment, but after the fighting began, Kalb decided he wanted to make his military fortune in America and by 1776 had begun to recruit French officers to join the cause.

In November 1776, Broglie arranged for Lafayette to meet with Kalb, who worked as a sort of middleman helping other French officers who wanted to go to America and fight the British. Lafayette met almost daily throughout that month with Kalb. Then, in early December, Kalb arranged a meeting with Silas Deane and his aide, William Carmichael. Deane, a Connecticut merchant and patriot, had been sent to Paris by the Continental Congress to secure French support for the fight against the British. Posing as merchants, Deane and Carmichael helped arrange significant shipments of money, cannons, muskets, ammunition, tents, and other military supplies—and French officers—to the American cause. The two Americans had to work in secret because the French did not want it known that they were helping the rebellious Americans.

"When I presented to Mr. Deane my boyish face, (for I was scarcely nineteen years of age) I spoke more of my ardor in the cause than of my experience," Lafayette wrote in his memoirs, "but I dwelt much upon the effect my departure would excite in France, and he signed our mutual agreement." As for Broglie, Lafayette later said, with a certain amount of naïveté or self-delusion, "[his] affectionate heart, when all his efforts to turn me from this project had proved in vain, entered into my views with even paternal tenderness."[15]

On December 7, 1776, the nineteen-year-old Frenchman signed a contract with Deane—who, like many colonial leaders, was a Mason—which they dictated to Kalb, who spoke excellent English and served as translator. During his discussions with Deane, Lafayette pushed hard to be given the rank of major general in the Continental Army. This was the same rank that Deane had offered Kalb, an experienced war veteran who was fifty-five years old. Lafayette argued that unless he received a high rank, he never would be able to convince his family—primarily his powerful father-in-law, the Duc d'Ayen—to allow him to go to America.

In the contract's addendum, Lafayette wrote, in part: "I offer myself, and promise to depart when and how Mr. Deane shall judge proper, to serve the United States with all possible zeal, without any pension or particular allowance, reserving to myself the liberty of returning to Europe when my family or my king shall recall me."[16]

The offer to fight without pay helped convince Deane to go along with the young man's demand for a high rank. Lafayette's "high birth, his alliances, the great dignities which his family hold at this court, his considerable estates in this realm, his personal merit, his reputation, his disinterestedness, and, above all, his zeal for the liberty of our provinces," Deane said in the agreement, "have only been able to engage me to promise him the rank of Major General in the name of the United States."[17]

CHAPTER 2

Ardor for the Cause

I shall purchase a ship to carry out your officers; we must feel confidence in the future, and it is especially in the hour of danger that I wish to share your fortune.

—Marquis de Lafayette to Silas Deane, December 1776[1]

JUST AS LAFAYETTE WAS MAKING FINAL PREPARATIONS FOR HIS JOURNEY to America, bad news of the war arrived from New York. After capturing Staten Island in June 1776, British general William Howe's 32,000 troops, supplemented by his brother Admiral Richard Howe's fleet of some 10,000 sailors, attacked the Continental Army's commander in chief George Washington and his roughly 20,000 troops on Long Island. General Howe methodically routed Washington, who had no naval forces and had to make do with a corps of mostly poorly trained militiamen. Washington and his men fled east to Manhattan Island at the end of August.

Howe, whose forces included large numbers of Hessians, attacked again on September 15, forcing the overwhelmed Washington into White Plains, just north of the city in Westchester County. By mid-November, Howe had pushed Washington out of White Plains. Then the British general captured the last two American strongholds in the New York City area, at Fort Washington in New York (near the present-day site of the George Washington Bridge) and Fort Lee, across the Hudson River in New Jersey. Washington and his badly defeated and depleted army retreated south into New Jersey.

In the four days it took the British to capture the two forts, Washington suffered more than 3,000 men killed, wounded, or taken prisoner and lost 46 cannons, 8,000 cannon shot, 400,000 cartridges, and 2,800 muskets.[2] The British then occupied all of New York City. Howe sent some troops into New Jersey just behind Washington and his overmatched army, which had dwindled to around 5,000 combat-ready men.

It was a low moment for the rebellious Americans—one of the lowest in what would be a long war for independence. "These are the times that try men's souls," Thomas Paine, an aide-de-camp to General Nathanael Greene, famously wrote of this period in his powerful political pamphlet *The Crisis* in late December 1776.

As Paine counseled "perseverance and fortitude," Washington's army was near collapse, and the war effort appeared doomed. Loyalists in New York and New Jersey openly flocked to the English cause, many of Washington's troops' tours of duty were about to expire, and politicians and other military leaders questioned their commander in chief's abilities after the fiasco in New York. Unless he could induce thousands of men to join the cause,

Washington wrote on December 18, "I think the game is pretty near up."[3]

✠

Word of these "very bad tidings," as Lafayette put it, reached France and gave his family more fodder for trying to talk the young man out of going to America.[4] Another factor in the family equation was Lafayette's wife, Adrienne. No one had consulted Adrienne on the matter of her husband crossing the Atlantic, and she was now pregnant with the young couple's second child. Making matters worse for Lafayette was the fact that the French government, fearing political consequences from England if it appeared that King Louis XVI was openly encouraging French soldiers to join the American rebels, decided to rescind its permission to allow another group of French soldiers to join the Continental Army. That contingent included Lafayette's brother-in-law, the Vicomte de Noailles.

Many would have caved in to all of this familial and governmental pressure. But all of these factors made Lafayette only more eager to join the rebellion.

"Until now, sir," Lafayette said he told Deane after hearing the bad news from New York, "you have only seen my ardour in your cause, and that may not prove at present wholly useless. I shall purchase a ship to carry out your officers; we must feel confidence in the future, and it is especially in the hour of danger that I wish to share your fortune."[5]

The rich, young Frenchman did indeed purchase a ship. With the help of an associate of Comte Charles-François de Broglie from the southwestern French port city of Bordeaux, Lafayette made arrangements to buy a 220-ton cargo vessel, *La Bonne Mère,* on February 11, 1777. The price: 112,000 livres. Lafayette put 40,000 livres down and promised to pay the balance by June.[6] The vessel, which he renamed *La Victoire,* had a crew of thirty and was equipped with two cannons.

Ten days later, Lafayette left France—not for the United States and not on *La Victoire.* Instead, at the insistence of his powerful father-in-law, the Duc d'Ayen, Lafayette took a small boat across the English Channel to pay a visit to his wife's uncle, the Marquis de Noailles, the French ambassador to England. Lafayette went unwillingly and only because he wanted to cooperate with his in-laws who pushed the London trip, or at least to give the appearance of cooperating. He felt that if he obeyed his influential father-in-law by first going to London, the Duc d'Ayen would be more inclined to allow his impetuous teenage son-in-law to go to America.

Lafayette had not yet learned English and met only a few French-speaking people in London. That included Horace Walpole and several English military men who had fought against the rebels in America. The latter group included General Henry Clinton, home on leave after helping General Howe rout Washington on Long Island. Lafayette's uncle, the ambassador, also presented the young man to King George III.

Lafayette hid his pro-American sympathies during his brief audience with the king and during his social conversation with Clinton, who would later take over as commander in chief of the British forces in America. But Lafayette did let several other Englishmen know his feelings about the revolt in the colonies.

"Whilst I concealed my intentions, I openly avowed my sentiments; I often defended the Americans," Lafayette said in his memoirs. "I rejoiced at their success at Trenton [on December 26, 1776]; and my spirit of opposition obtained for me an invitation to breakfast with Lord Shelbourne."[7] That was the pro-American politician, the Earl of Shelburne, who coincidentally had fought at the Battle of Minden, where Lafayette's father died, in the Seven Years' War.

Lafayette spent three mostly unhappy weeks in London. On March 9, 1777, he wrote a letter to his father-in-law in which the young man continued to state his case for going across the Atlantic to fight the British. "I have found a unique opportunity to distinguish myself and to learn my profession," he said. "I am a general officer in the army of the United States of America. My zeal for their cause and my sincerity have won their confidence. For my part, I have done all that I can for them, and their interests will always be dearer to me than my own."[8] Lafayette said the prospect of going to America filled him with joy "at having found so beautiful a chance to accomplish something and to learn."[9]

Lafayette left London, and upon arriving in France, he stayed incognito for a few days at Johan de Kalb's house in Paris. It was during this time that the wealthy young man completed the purchase of *La Victoire,* borrowing money from friends so his father-in-law wouldn't realize what was going on. Kalb, Broglie, and Lafayette also decided on the final roster of French officers who would accompany them on the journey, and Silas Deane signed off on a list of thirteen names.

Deane's aide, William Carmichael, provided letters of introduction to several members of the Continental Congress for Lafayette and Kalb. Deane also gave them letters of introduction to three of the highest American officials: Continental Army commander in chief George Washington; the influential financier Robert Morris, a member of the Committee of Secret Correspondence, which oversaw Deane's procurement work in France; and John Hancock, president of the Second Continental Congress. All the letters took note of Lafayette's wealth and powerful, well-connected family.

Without a word to his pregnant wife or other family members, Lafayette took off from Paris to Bordeaux with the group, arriving by coach on March 19. By doing so, he all but created an international incident. His in-laws were outraged when they found out he had left Paris. The Duc d'Ayen showed up at Versailles, where he demanded that the Comte de Vergennes, Louis XVI's minister of foreign affairs, do something to stop the boat from sailing.

Vergennes was equally perturbed, fearing that the mission could lead to war with Britain. Certainly, allowing Lafayette to go and fight with the Americans was at the very least a slap in the face to the British. This was especially so considering that the young marquis had so recently been introduced to King George III by the French ambassador, knowing full well that he would soon be taking part in mortal combat against the king's men.

At Vergennes' urging and to try to save face, Louis XVI issued an order forbidding any French officers from serving in America. And, singling out the son-in-law of the Duc d'Ayen by name, the king ordered all French fighters en route to or already in America to return home—or as he put it: "notably Monsieur le Marquis de la Fayette, to leave immediately and return to France."[10]

The orders never were carried out. What's more, when word got out in Paris and elsewhere in France that Lafayette and company were heading for America, the marquis became something of a folk hero, especially among other youthful French military officers and young women. Some went as far as importuning the d'Ayen family to give their blessing to their son-in-law, something that was not lost on the English spies in Paris.

"The ladies reproach the parents [in-law] of M. de Lafayette for having tried to stop such a noble enterprise," the English ambassador in Paris, Lord Stormont, wrote to the British Foreign Office. "One of the ladies even declared, 'If the Duc d'Ayen thwarts his son-in-law in such a project, he should not expect to marry the rest of his daughters.'"[11]

✦

When Lafayette and crew arrived in Bordeaux, the *Victoire* was not ready to leave port. Lafayette spent a few days more or less in hiding with the Marshal de Mouchy, his wife's great-uncle. When it came time to register with the government officials charged with emigration matters, Lafayette signed in as "Gilbert du Motier, Chevalier [Knight] de Chavaillac," the latter an old spelling of his home village. He listed his physical description as tall, blond, and twenty years old. In fact, the six-feet-tall marquis' hair was still more red than blond, and he wouldn't see his twentieth birthday for six months.

The *Victoire* set sail down the Garonne River on March 25, reaching the port of Bordeaux the next day. Only a few hours later, a courier from Paris arrived in the city with the king's order. When word reached Paris that Lafayette had made his escape, many people cheered the news.

"It's undoubtedly an act of folly," a French noblewoman wrote to Horace Walpole on March 31, "but one which does him no dishonor and which, on the contrary, is characterized by courage and the desire for glory. People praise him more than they blame him."[12]

The Duc d'Ayen, concerned primarily with his son-in-law's safety should he fall into British hands, wrote a letter to Lafayette, telling him how unhappy the family—and King Louis XVI—were with him and ordering him to call off the venture. The duke also had Deane prepare letters to George Washington and John Hancock, asking them to send the young man back home to France.

Meanwhile, things were not going well aboard the *Victoire*. On March 28, at the small port of Los Pasajes, outside the Spanish coastal city of San Sebastian, Lafayette began having serious second thoughts, mainly about his family's reaction to his departure. He ordered the ship to stay at anchor until he received word from his father-in-law. While the ship sat there, a courier from the king arrived with an order commanding Lafayette to go to Marseilles to meet his in-laws, who would arrive soon thereafter before setting off on a tour of Italy.

That was not news Lafayette wanted to hear. So he decided to go back to France and set things straight with the Duc d'Ayen. Kalb was unhappy about that but was in no position to order the boat to set sail because he did not own the vessel. Kalb had dinner with Lafayette in San Sebastian, after which Lafayette announced his intention to return to Bordeaux.

"At this moment, he has abandoned his trip to America and recanted his lust for war," Kalb wrote to his wife on April 1. "He has left for Bordeaux and from there he wants to go to Paris....I do not think he will return, and I advised him to sell the ship."[13]

Lafayette arrived in Bordeaux on April 3. He reported to the commandant of the port, asking his permission to go to Paris to see his wife and family. The commandant told him, instead, to go meet his in-laws in Marseilles. Lafayette refused and wrote to the court in Versailles pleading his case.

With the entire mission up in the air, the Comte de Broglie—perhaps the most influential person in France who desperately wanted Lafayette to go to America—took action. Broglie sent a trusted aide, the Vicomte de Mauroy, from Paris to Bordeaux to try to talk Lafayette into getting back on the ship. When Mauroy arrived, he told Lafayette that the French government actually wanted him and other officers to go to the colonies to fight the English but couldn't say so publicly for diplomatic reasons. He also said that, despite rumors, the king would not prosecute Lafayette if he went back to Spain and set sail for America. That, plus the information (also via Mauroy from Broglie) that Lafayette's in-laws were the only ones who wanted him to stay home, convinced the marquis to change his mind once again, and he set out for Spain.

To throw off the French emigration officials, Lafayette and Mauroy took a coach headed in the opposite direction of Bordeaux, toward Marseilles. Soon after they departed, they stopped the carriage, and Lafayette mounted a horse and began galloping in the opposite direction toward Bayonne. He was in disguise, dressed as a courier. The young marquis made it to the ship in the harbor on April 17. Three days later, on April 20, 1777, the *Victoire* set sail for America.

❖

The journey across the Atlantic took two months. Lafayette was seasick for most of the first few weeks. When he finally gained his sea legs, the marquis found life on board extremely tedious. "I have been in the most boring country," Lafayette wrote to Adrienne. "The sea looks so morose that I believe we make each other sad. Here days follow one another and, even worse, look alike. Always the sky, always the water, and the following day it is the same."[14]

To counter the boredom, Lafayette filled the hours learning English and studying military strategy and tactics with the help of Kalb and the veteran French soldiers on board. He also spent many days writing a long letter to his wife. It was full of expressions of love and longing—and commitment to his self-ascribed mission. Lafayette spoke of the "awful emotion" he experienced as he sailed away and how he would miss Adrienne, his friends, and his daughter. He asked Adrienne to forgive him for defying her father's wishes.[15]

The young man then went on to predict what life would be like once he took part in the war against the British, downplaying the danger, saying that he would have seen much more combat action had he stayed at home in the French Army. "The position of general officer has always been considered as an assurance of immortality," he said. "It is a service so different from what I would have done in France, as a colonel for example."[16]

Lafayette told his wife that as a general, he envisioned himself giving "counseling only" and would not run any risk. He said he could prove that he was telling the truth because "at present we are in some danger for we could be attacked by British vessels and mine is not equipped to defend itself. But once we have arrived, I will be perfectly safe."[17]

Continuing the letter on June 7, Lafayette spoke in the loftiest of idealistic tones about the reasons he had decided to join the fight. "Defender of this freedom which I venerate, freer than anyone and coming as a friend to offer our help to such an interesting republic, I bring here my integrity and good will only. No ambition, no personal interests."[18]

❖

As the *Victoire* neared the blockaded harbor of Charleston, South Carolina, tensions rose aboard ship. The captain sailed without lights. The men were spooked by every ship sighting in the distance, fearing imminent attack by British cruisers. Food and water ran low.

Close to Charleston, the crew had a serious scare when a small boat approached. "At forty leagues from shore, they were met by a small vessel: the captain turned pale," Lafayette wrote of himself in his memoirs. "It turned out, fortunately, to be an American ship, whom they vainly endeavoured to keep up with; but scarcely had the former lost sight of M. de Lafayette's vessel, when it fell in with two English frigates."[19]

The American captain warned the *Victoire* about the British ships, and its captain avoided them by heading north along the South Carolina coast. On Friday, June 13, 1777, after fifty-six days at sea, the crew spotted a small harbor about sixty miles north of Charleston at Georgetown Bay. Lafayette, Kalb, and several crew members climbed into the ship's small launch and headed toward shore that afternoon to find help to get into the harbor. After rowing for hours, they ran into a small oyster boat manned by slaves owned by Major Benjamin Huger of the South Carolina militia. Following the boat to shore, Lafayette and company set foot on American soil for the first time just before midnight on North Island in the marshes along Huger's plantation summer home.

The unexpected arrival startled Huger and his household, but after Kalb made it known that they were French officers, Huger accepted them with open arms. "I have arrived, my Dear Heart, and in very good health, at the house of an American officer. Imagine my joy!" Lafayette wrote to his wife the next day. "The countryside is open and there is no fighting, at least not much. Manners in this world are simple, honest and, in all things, worthy of the country where the beautiful word liberty resonates."[20]

Lafayette had a plan: "From Charles town I will go to Philadelphia by land and then join the army."[21]

CHAPTER 3

Bleeding in the Cause

Gilbert Motier de Lafayette—the son of the victim of Minden; and he is bleeding in the cause of North American Independence and of Freedom.

—John Quincy Adams, December 31, 1834[1]

IT TOOK LAFAYETTE AND COMPANY THREE DAYS AND TWO NIGHTS TO reach Charleston, South Carolina. Their reception on June 16, 1777, was underwhelming. "The people of Charleston, like all the people of this part of the continent, detest the French and heap abuse on them," Charles-François Dubuysson, one of Lafayette's fellow officers, wrote in his journal.[2] The citizens still harbored anti-French feelings from the bitter fighting during the French and Indian War, which had ended fourteen years earlier. The resentment also stemmed from the increasing number of French citizens, primarily from Martinique, posing as experienced military men who arrived in the city to volunteer for the cause.

But the people of Charleston changed their minds about these particular Frenchmen when the well-provisioned *Victoire* pulled into Charleston's harbor the following day. Charleston residents began to realize just who the youthful marquis was. Once they found out that he was a wealthy, well-connected nobleman, the city fathers treated Lafayette and company like visiting royalty. They proudly showed their guests the sights and treated them to a lavish dinner with, among others, General William Moultrie, who had defeated the British fleet in a nine-hour battle in Charleston Harbor on June 28, 1776.

Lafayette was so impressed with General Moultrie, a fellow Mason, that he donated arms, uniforms, and equipment to the South Carolina militia in his honor. Moultrie and the other South Carolina generals, Lafayette said in his memoirs, received him "with the utmost kindness and attention." "The new works were shown [to him] and also that battery which Moultrie afterwards defended so extremely well, and which the English appear, we must acknowledge, to have seized the only possible means of destroying."[3]

Several days later, on June 26, 1777, Lafayette, Johan de Kalb, and five other French officers set out for the colonial capital of Philadelphia, more than 600 miles to the north. Lafayette portrayed the trip through rose-colored glasses when writing about it decades later in his memoirs. He wrote about learning the language and customs of the residents of South Carolina, North Carolina, Virginia, and Maryland on the journey, and observing "new productions of nature, and new methods of cultivation." Vast forests, he said, "and immense rivers combine to give to that country an appearance of youth and majesty."[4]

In fact, the trip had been extremely arduous and vexing, and it took nearly a month to complete. During the trek, wagons broke down, horses fell ill and died, and the intense heat and humidity hit the Frenchmen particularly hard, since they were not used to the climate. They were beset by gnats and mosquitoes and sickened by dysentery and fevers. With all their horses gone, the men wound up walking into Philadelphia on Sunday, July 27, 1777.

As one of the French officers wrote in his journal: "We endured abominable heat in South Carolina, and at the end of each day we had to endure detestable water. . . . People are not very obliging, and we find assistance only by paying for it. . . . On the whole, the French are very poorly repaid here for their sacrifices on behalf of an ungrateful and undeserving people."[5]

Things improved a bit for the Frenchmen after they marched into Philadelphia. The men presented their papers to John Hancock, who sent them to the prominent financier Robert Morris. The letter from Silas Deane asked Morris to act as a surrogate father to Lafayette and explained how important and influential his family was, describing the good that these new allies could bring to the American cause.

"A generous reception of him will do us infinite service," Deane wrote. "He is above pecuniary considerations. All he seeks is glory, and every one here says he has taken the most noble method to procure it. You may think it makes a great noise in Europe and at the same time see that well managed it will greatly help us."[6]

Lafayette had other influential people in his corner as well. Benjamin Franklin, who had arrived in Paris to lobby for French military and economic aid just before Lafayette left, had written to the colonies on the young man's behalf. Franklin's letter to George Washington also stressed the benefits to the American cause if Washington allowed the French general to serve in his army. Giving Lafayette a military commission, Franklin wrote, would be "an act of benevolence gratefully remembered and acknowledged by a number of worthy persons in France who interest themselves extremely in the welfare of the amiable young nobleman."[7]

Back home, Lafayette's in-laws had changed their tune, perhaps because so many influential people in France made it known publicly that they looked upon the marquis as a hero. That group included Franklin, as well as the eighty-three-year-old Voltaire, the famed French poet and philosopher; Horace Walpole; and the esteemed English historian Edward Gibbon.

Back in Philadelphia on July 27, Morris told Lafayette and company to report the next day to Independence Hall, where the Continental Congress would be meeting. The reception there, however, was not a good one. The Frenchmen were refused admittance into the august assembly and unceremoniously told to wait outside on the street. When Morris and Massachusetts Delegate James Lovell finally came out to greet them, they delivered unpromising news.

Lovell "received us in the street," Charles-François Dubuysson reported, "where he left us, after calling us adventurers—in very good French.... 'French officers are very forward to come and serve us without being asked. Last year we did lack officers, but this year we have plenty and all of them are experienced.' Such was our reception by Congress. We did not know what to think. It is impossible to be more astounded than we were."[8]

Lafayette may have been astounded, but he remained upbeat. He came up with a solution to the rebuff: to write a note to Lovell and the Continental Congress expressing his zeal for the cause and his willingness to lend his talents. It read: "After the sacrifices I have made, I have the right to exact two favours: one is, to serve at my own expense—the other is, to serve at first as volunteer."[9]

The offer worked. The next day, Lovell sought out Lafayette, apologized, and announced that he would be appointed a volunteer major general assigned to Washington's staff. Kalb and several other French officers also received Congress's blessing to join the Continental Army, and a few other French officers were assigned to Lafayette to serve as his aides-de-camp—at the marquis' expense.

The nineteen-year-old received his major general's sash on July 31. Five days later at a dinner, Lafayette met George Washington, who had come to Philadelphia to brief members of the Continental Congress on the precarious state of military affairs (the British were moving toward the city). The two men bonded almost immediately. By all accounts, the forty-five-year-old, childless Washington was taken by the young man's ebullience and seemingly profound dedication to the American cause, as well as the fact that he was a fellow Mason. Lafayette simply stood in awe of the American commander in chief.

"Although he was surrounded by officers and citizens, it was impossible to mistake for a moment his majestic figure and deportment; nor was he less distinguished by the noble affability of his manner," Lafayette wrote in his memoirs of that first encounter.[10]

After dinner, Washington, to Lafayette's delight, asked the Frenchman to accompany him on an inspection of the city's defenses and then welcomed him to the cause. Lafayette later wrote about it in the loftiest of tones, made even loftier by his use of the third person in referring to himself:

> The majesty of [Washington's] figure and his height were unmistakable. His affable and noble welcome to M. de Lafayette was no less distinguished, and M. de Lafayette accompanied him on his inspections. The General invited him to establish himself in his house [i.e., on his staff], and from that moment he looked upon it as his own. It was with such simplicity that two friends were united whose attachment and confidence were cemented by the greatest of causes.[11]

At this point in the war, more than two years after Lexington and Concord, British troops were securely ensconced in bases in New York and in Newport, Rhode Island. British General William Howe had devised a new plan in the wake of the embarrassing defeat on

December 26, 1776, at Trenton. It was there that his Hessian troops were taken by surprise by Washington after the famed crossing of the Delaware, which led to an American victory on January 3, 1777, at Princeton. Howe decided to amass a large number of troops to take the capital of Philadelphia, where he believed many Loyalists would welcome the British after they routed the rebels. Sir George Germain, Britain's secretary of state for the colonies, approved Howe's plan in March.

Washington benefited during this war hiatus when significant numbers of volunteers signed up to fight the British. During this time, too, Franklin and Deane had convinced the French government to send large amounts of supplies to the Americans. The first secret shiploads of material aid arrived in the spring and summer of 1777.

This was also the time when experienced French and other foreign military men began to join the cause. The list included the French general Louis du Portail, who took over as the army's chief engineer; Thaddeus Kosciuszko, a Polish officer and an accomplished military engineer; the veteran Polish general Casimir Pulaski, who had been with Washington since the summer of 1775 and organized the Continental Army's first well-trained cavalry contingent; and the self-proclaimed "baron" Friedrich Wilhelm von Steuben, who would arrive in 1778—a German veteran of the Seven Years' War recruited by Franklin and Deane.

These and other experienced European officers brought a measure of professionalism to Washington's army. Still, when Lafayette met Washington at the end of July 1777, the Continental Army was made up primarily of what it had been since the fighting began: a relatively untrained group of inexperienced but dedicated enlistees.

The defenses around Philadelphia that Lafayette inspected with Washington were strung along the Delaware River. Washington also had the city's ports blocked. Therefore, Howe decided to make a long run around the defenses and attack Philadelphia from the south. He put most of his 13,000-man army on ships, which sailed down the Atlantic coast, then turned back up the Chesapeake Bay heading north. About a month after they set out, the troops landed on the inner tip of the Chesapeake Bay at the port town of Head of Elk (now North East, near Elkton), Maryland, some fifty-five miles south of Philadelphia. When Washington discovered on August 22 that Howe would be attacking from the south, he began moving his troops about thirty miles west of the city to positions along Brandywine Creek just north of Wilmington, Delaware, in the hamlet of Chadds Ford, Pennsylvania.

⊕

Lafayette had spent lavishly in Philadelphia preparing to go to war for the first time. He bought a carriage; horses; and all manner of arms, equipment, and uniforms for himself and his two aides (whose salaries he paid), Jean-Joseph Sourbader de Gimat and Louis Saint Ange Morel, Chevalier de La Colombe. The three French officers arrived at Washington's headquarters about twenty miles north of Philadelphia on August 19. On August 24, Washington marched his 10,000 troops through the streets of the fledgling nation's capital, with Lafayette at his side to boost morale and let the local Tories see the large number of men he had under arms.

Lafayette had good things to say about the fighting ability of the troops. "The soldiers were fine, and the officers zealous; virtue stood in place of science, and each day added both to experience and discipline."[12] Washington decided to get a personal look at Howe's troops. On August 26, he set out on horseback south from Philadelphia. He took along his top commander, General Nathanael Greene, a small group of guards, as well as his young French protégé. Aside from being forced by a severe thunderstorm to spend the night in a farmhouse close to the British camp, nothing much happened on that reconnaissance mission, other than the fact that Washington showed his admiration for Lafayette by asking him to participate in the mission.

On September 8, two days after Lafayette's twentieth birthday, the British troops, now recovered after an arduous month at sea, began to move toward Philadelphia. The Battle of Brandywine began on the morning of September 11, 1777.

A dense fog had burned off by mid-morning, and the day turned hot and humid. In a fight that, with some 25,000 combatants involved, would be the largest of the Revolutionary War, Washington divided his army into two parts. He commanded troops at Chadds Ford, and General John Sullivan protected his right flank upstream with several thousand men.

Howe had the commander in chief of the German troops in America, General Wilhelm von Knyphausen, and his 5,000 Hessian troops stage a mock attack with artillery on Washington's position. He did it to cover the fact that at the same time, Howe had General Charles Cornwallis and his 8,000 men march fifteen miles north and cross the Brandywine to outflank the Americans. Sullivan, hit from behind, was forced to retreat.

When Lafayette, standing with Washington under the mock bombardment at Chadds Ford, learned of Cornwallis's attack, he all but begged the general to be allowed to join the fray. Washington gave his permission, and Lafayette, sword at his side, galloped off into the first battle of his life.

By the time he arrived with his two aides, Gimat and La Colombe, Lafayette said in his memoirs, "the enemy had crossed the ford. Sullivan's troops had barely enough time to form a line in front of a thin wood." After enduring a "murderous barrage" of enemy cannon and musket fire, "the entire right and left side buckled."[13] At that point, the American troops turned and ran. The twenty-year-old Frenchman, in his first experience under fire, acted like a battle-hardened veteran. He rallied the retreating troops by yelling at them from his horse, and then he dismounted and physically pushed them toward the enemy. Many men did return to the fight. But they soon were overwhelmed again, and Lafayette ordered them to fall back into an orderly retreat.

Washington averted complete disaster at Brandywine by sending 1,300 men under General Greene to fight a rearguard action. Still, the Americans suffered some 1,300 casualties (killed, wounded, or captured), while Howe had less than 600. The overwhelmed Americans retreated to Chester, Pennsylvania, twelve miles from the battlefield.

Only when Lafayette ordered the retreat did he realize he had been wounded. A musket ball had gone through his left calf during the fight, and his boot filled with blood. Although not life threatening, the wound was severe enough that Gimat and La Colombe had to lift him onto his horse.

Lafayette stayed on his horse, accompanying the retreating men to Chester. Soon after arriving, Washington joined them and had his surgeon treat the wounded marquis. Lafayette was taken to the nearby Birmingham Church, where James Monroe looked after him. The future president, who spoke French, kept up Lafayette's spirits, and the two formed what would become a long, close friendship.

The next day, Lafayette was loaded onto a boat on the Delaware to receive better medical care in Philadelphia. Lafayette wrote in his memoirs that as he was led away, he heard Washington say, "Treat him as if he were my son."[14]

In a letter to his wife the next day, Lafayette downplayed the wound, telling Adrienne that the musket ball "hurt my leg a little, but…the ball touched neither a bone nor a nerve, and I will have to stay in bed for only a little while."[15] Henry Laurens, a Continental Congress delegate from South Carolina, took an interest in Lafayette and arranged to have him sent on September 21 to Moravian Community Hospital in Bethlehem, Pennsylvania, about fifty miles north of Philadelphia. Laurens, who would later succeed John Hancock as president of the Continental Congress, had a son, Lieutenant Colonel John Laurens, on Washington's staff at Brandywine.

During the weeks that he spent recovering in Bethlehem, Lafayette worked on improving his English and did a lot of reading. He devoured many of the works of the eighteenth-century French and French-influenced *philosophes*—Enlightenment thinkers such as John-Jacques Rousseau and the Baron Montesquieu, who propounded modern political and religious ideas. Lafayette also wrote a long stream of letters, including one to Washington on October 14, strongly hinting that he was ready to leave his staff job and take command of a fighting division of American troops.

Writing "with all the confidence of a son, of a friend, as you favoured me with those two so precious titles," Lafayette spoke of his respect and affection for Washington. The marquis then made his case for taking over one of Washington's divisions. "I know it is not right," Lafayette said, "but I would deserve the reproaches of my friends and family if I would leave the advantages of mine to stay in a country where I could not find the occasions of distinguishing myself."[16]

Before he received an answer from Washington, Lafayette decided he was well enough to return to battle. On October 18, he managed to saddle up and ride his horse to Washington's new headquarters at Whitemarsh, about twenty miles north of Philadelphia. Lafayette soon became fast friends with generals Nathanael Greene and John Sullivan, and Daniel Morgan, a colonel of the Eleventh Virginia Regiment. Morgan, a grizzled veteran of the French and Indian War, had been fighting the British since the Revolutionary War broke out.

Lafayette also sent letters back to France, urging his nation's leaders to back the American cause and, if necessary, wage all-out war against England. This flurry of correspondence included missives to Foreign Minister Comte de Vergennes and Prime Minister Comte de Maurepas, in which Lafayette argued that France should attack the British throughout their far-flung empire in the West Indies, Canada,

India, and elsewhere in Asia. Maurepas did not react favorably to that fanciful proposal, saying that what Lafayette wanted to do would require that France "sell all the furniture at Versailles to underwrite the American cause."[17]

But Vergennes was impressed by what he heard from Lafayette, as well as by the news that the Americans under General Horatio Gates had crushed British General John Burgoyne at Saratoga, New York, on October 17. The British defeat boosted morale significantly in the colonies. As for Lafayette, Vergennes recognized the importance of the marquis' close relationships with some of the most influential Americans, especially Washington, Hancock, and Laurens.

Lafayette's success in America all but ended Comte Charles-François de Broglie's plan to come and take over the fight against the British. Vergennes already had Lafayette—a man on the ground who was close to the American leadership, who had literally shed blood in the American cause and was dedicated to working against France's longtime enemy, England. Broglie never left for America.

❖

On November 1, 1777, George Washington, despite some misgivings, gave in to Lafayette's wishes (and to those of Greene, who lobbied for his new French friend) and sent a letter to Congress recommending that Lafayette be given command of a division of troops. In the letter, Washington praised Lafayette for pushing the American cause to Vergennes and Maurepas. "In all his letters [he] has placed our affairs in the best situation he could," Washington wrote. The young Frenchman, Washington reported, was "sensible—discreet in manners—has made great proficiency in our language, and from the disposition he discovered at the Battle of Brandywine, possesses a large share of bravery and military ardor."[18]

Before Congress took action, Lafayette again proved himself to be a bold, courageous leader under fire. On November 20, despite the fact that his leg wound had not yet healed, he volunteered to join a large raiding party under Nathanael Greene that went after Cornwallis's camp in New Jersey. After ferrying across the Delaware River and embarking at Burlington, New Jersey, Greene arrayed his troops in a defensive position. Greene gave Lafayette command of some 350 of his 3,000 men and ordered him on November 25 to find the camp, which he believed to be in Haddonfield, about ten miles east.

Lafayette had under his command some 200 of Daniel Morgan's famed riflemen, fresh from their triumph at Saratoga, along with two companies of New Jersey militiamen. The party ran into a picket force of Cornwallis's Hessians near Gloucester. Lafayette did not hesitate, ordering his men to charge the enemy. They routed the Hessians, then frontally attacked their camp, defended by roughly 350 enemy troops and two cannons. When the smoke cleared, Lafayette had vanquished the enemy, which suffered sixty casualties to just six for the Americans—one killed and five wounded.

Greene was especially pleased with what Lafayette had accomplished in just his second engagement. The Rhode Islander praised the Frenchman for his daring and effective leadership under fire. Greene wrote to Washington: "The Marquis is determined to be in the way of danger."[19]

When Washington received that report, he sent a second message to Congress singing Lafayette's praises and requested again that he be given a division to command. "I am convinced," Washington wrote, "he possesses a large share of that military ardor which generally characterizes the nobility of his country. He went to Jersey with Genl. Greene, and I find that he has not been inactive there."[20]

Congress, with Laurens also putting in a good word, agreed, and on December 4, 1777, George Washington announced that the Marquis de Lafayette could choose a division to command. Lafayette, showing his growing admiration for Washington, picked one from Virginia, Washington's home state. It had been led by Major General

Adam Stephen, a rival of Washington's dating from the French and Indian War, who had been court-martialed after his recent less-than-inspiring performances at Brandywine and the fighting at Germantown.

Lafayette could not have been happier with the assignment, and news from home buoyed his enthusiasm. In a parcel of letters he received on November 28 came word that his wife had given birth to his second daughter, Anastasie-Louise-Pauline, on July 1. Lafayette would not learn until several months later that his older daughter, Henriette, had died soon after the birth of her sister.

❖

After his decisive September 11 victory at Brandywine, General Howe had taken his time and did not march into Philadelphia until September 26. His men and the British naval forces soon destroyed the American forts along the Delaware River and opened the city to British shipping. Howe positioned about 9,000 of his troops at Germantown north of the city, 3,000 in New Jersey, and several thousand in the city itself.

As winter arrived, Howe had reason to be optimistic. He had taken the American rebels' capital city, a fact that he believed would significantly dampen his enemy's morale. Howe also thought that many local Loyalists would support him. And he was sure that when spring came, he would put an end to the rebellion itself. Settling in to wait for warmer weather, Howe famously brought his mistress, Elizabeth Loring, from New York to keep him company.

The Continental Congress had abandoned the city on September 18, moving the national capital, for one day, to Lancaster, Pennsylvania, and then to York, about a hundred miles west of Philadelphia. Washington decided to spend the winter in a small hamlet about twenty miles northwest of Philadelphia: a place called Valley Forge.

CHAPTER 4

A Trustworthy Friend

It is in a camp in the middle of woods; it is fifteen hundred leagues from you that I find myself buried in midwinter.

—Marquis de Lafayette to his wife, Adrienne, January 6, 1778[1]

THE MARQUIS DE LAFAYETTE SPENT MOST OF DECEMBER 1777 AND January 1778 with General George Washington and his 6,000 Continental Army troops, who set up winter quarters at Valley Forge, Pennsylvania. During that long winter, the ill-equipped Americans suffered severe hardships. Some went barefoot. Others didn't have blankets to sleep under. Food was scarce. Sufficient supplies rarely made it to the camp. And hundreds died after suffering from diseases such as influenza, typhus, typhoid fever, and dysentery.

By early February 1778, Washington had all but lost hope about the supply situation. "The occasional deficiencies in the Article of Provisions, which we have often severely felt, seem now on the point of resolving themselves into this fatal Crisis, total want and a dissolution of the Army," he wrote to William Buchanan, his less-than-efficient commissary general.[2]

All was not lost, though. By early March, Nathanael Greene took charge of the Quartermaster Corps, and the supply situation improved markedly. The Continental Army also benefited from a new training regimen put in place by the veteran Prussian general Friedrich Wilhelm von Steuben, who arrived at Valley Forge in February 1778 and became inspector general in charge of training. By springtime, von Steuben had taught Washington's men European battle formations and movements. The Continental Army had been reorganized and revitalized.

＋

As for Lafayette, the young French general basked in his elevation to the post of division commander. Lafayette freely spent his own money to buy uniforms and muskets for his troops, and he lived among them during the coldest part of the winter. He never wavered in his enthusiasm for the cause or his devotion to George Washington, even when his wife's family strongly hinted that he had paid his dues in America and it was time to come home.

Lafayette proved his steadfast loyalty to Washington during the Valley Forge encampment by doing everything in his power to help his commander in chief thwart the so-called Conway Cabal, a never-hatched military-political plot aimed at forcing Washington to give up command of the Continental Army. The cabal came to nothing, but for a few weeks—from mid-December 1777 to late January 1778—rumors swirled in the Continental Congress in York and at Valley Forge about a power struggle for control of the army. The plot, such as it was, centered on Irish-born Thomas Conway, who had served in the French and Prussian armies and had come to the United States the previous spring through the offices of Silas Deane in Paris. The Continental Congress had appointed him a brigadier general, and he went on to fight in the battles of Brandywine and Germantown.

The affair also included a plan Conway devised to move Lafayette far away from Valley Forge. Conway convinced the American Board of War (led by General Horatio Gates) on January 28, 1778, to appoint Lafayette to command the Northern Army of the United States, ordering him to take that army north, invade Canada, and return that territory to France. Lafayette had discussions with the War Board in York and with Washington in Valley Forge. Neither man liked the situation; both only agreed reluctantly.

Lafayette asked for and received a series of concessions from Congress before he would accept the order to go north. These included details, in writing, of the invasion plan and the power to appoint his own officers. He also insisted that all his orders come from his hero, George Washington, not through Congress via the Board of War. Lafayette chose twenty French officers for his staff, including his two loyal aides, Jean-Joseph Sourbader de Gimat and Louis Saint Ange Morel, Chevalier de La Colombe. That group also included the French engineer Captain Pierre L'Enfant, who would go on in 1791 to lay out the design of the city of Washington, D.C. Lafayette also insisted that Johan de Kalb be his second in command, not Conway as Congress suggested.

His January 31 written orders from Gates for this "irruption into Canada" directed Lafayette to make haste. "As success will depend principally upon the vigour, and the alertness with which the Enterprise is conducted, the Board recommended it to you to lose no time," Gates said. "The rapidity of your motions and the consternation of the enemy will do the business."[3]

Gates ordered Lafayette to strike either at Montreal or St. Johns (now Saint-Jean, northeast of Québec city), to try to convince Canadians to join the American cause, to attack the enemy, and then head south to Saratoga. The expedition's main objective was to take Montreal and confiscate British arms, ammunition, and other war materiel, as well as any supplies such as linens and Indian goods that Lafayette could find.

✦

The marquis headed north in the dead of winter, leaving York on February 3. Six days later, he wrote to Washington from Flemington, New Jersey, describing what had become a very difficult mission. "I go on very slowly sometimes pierced by rain, sometimes covered with snow, and not thinking many handsome thoughts about the projected *incursion* into Canada," Lafayette said.[4] As he proceeded, Lafayette and his small contingent ran into other weather-related obstacles, including the wide and deep Susquehanna River, which, Lafayette wrote in his memoirs, he and his men crossed only after avoiding "floating masses of ice." [5]

When Lafayette and his men arrived at Albany, New York, on February 17, they were not exactly happy with what they saw. Instead of a force of 2,500 men as Gates promised, Lafayette found fewer than 1,200. Nor did the promised supplies materialize. The troops, moreover, complained openly and bitterly about not being paid or provisioned properly. "Clothes, provisions, magazines, sledges, all were insufficient for that glacial expedition," Lafayette noted in his memoirs. [6]

"I have been (shamefully) deceived by the board of war," Lafayette wrote to Washington from Albany on February 19. "I was to find [General John] Stark with a large body" of troops, Lafayette said. "Well, the first letter I receive in Albany is from Gen. Stark who wishes to know what number of men, from where, for which time, for which rendezvous I desire him to rise."[7]

The trip was turning into a fiasco, and Lafayette realized it. He wrote what he called "a calm letter to Congress" on February 20, saying he would abandon the mission. "You will see very plainly that if proper orders [and] proper money had been sent some time ago, we could have been able to carry the expedition," Lafayette wrote. "I have found a great dissatisfaction among the troops owing to the want of clothes and money which could be attended with dangerous circumstances. That same want of money has thrown many departments in confusion and stopped their operations." Everyone in the army he had spoken to, Lafayette said, told him that the mission was doomed, and nothing he could do would save it.[8]

When word reached York that Gates's operation was dead in its tracks, nearly all of the anti-Washington sentiment in Congress ended. Gates's Board of War likewise lost support and never again became a factor in the war.

With the Canada invasion aborted, Lafayette decided to put his time in New York to good use. "I think it is my duty to mind the business of this part of America as well as I can," he wrote to Washington.[9]

The marquis set up a training and drilling regimen for his underpaid and underclothed troops in Albany. His old friend Kalb proved useful in that endeavor, boosting his morale and working effectively with the raw troops. After receiving $200,000 from Congress, Lafayette went about paying the army's debts to local merchants, buying clothes for the troops, and stocking up on materiel for whatever campaign would come next.

Lafayette also reached out to the local Indian tribes (the Oneida, Tuscarora, and Onondaga), hoping to persuade them to join the fight against the English. Early in March, he sat down with tribal elders in Johnstown, New York, and convinced at least some of them to pledge themselves to the anti-British cause.

Lafayette spent a total of six weeks in Albany. He worked with the Indians, drilled his troops, paid the bills, and fired off countless letters at night and sometimes in the early morning hours. He also worked industriously to shore up and obtain provisions for the forts that guarded the small towns in the area from British attacks. And he arranged several exchanges of sick and wounded prisoners with the British.

All the while, Lafayette industriously lobbied Congress to assign him to a new division and issue orders for him to attack the British in New York. "After such a noise made on account of my commanding an army," Lafayette wrote to his friend Henry Laurens on February 23, "I expect and wish much to be put in a separate command to do something."[10]

Those orders to attack the British never came. But Congress, in a conciliatory mood after the Conway fiasco and aware of Lafayette's passionate attachment to Washington, all but issued a formal apology to him on March 2.

The apology came in the form of a congressional resolution, which read: "It appears from authentic accounts that difficulties attend the prosecution of the irruption ordered to be made into Canada under the conduct of the Marquis de la Fayette, which render the attempt not only hazardous in a high degree but extremely imprudent." The resolution ordered the Board of War to "instruct the Marquis de la Fayette to suspend for the present the intended irruption, and at the same time, inform him that Congress entertain a high sense of his prudence, activity and zeal, and that they are fully persuaded nothing has, or would have been wanting on his part... to give the expedition the utmost possible effect."[11]

Then, on March 13, Congress issued orders returning the marquis and Kalb to the main army in Pennsylvania. Washington wrote to Lafayette a week later telling him of the orders and saying he wanted Lafayette "without loss of time [to] return to camp, to resume the command of a division of this Army."[12]

Lafayette wrote back pledging, not for the first or last time, his eternal loyalty to Washington. "I have given up on the idea of New York and my only desire is to join you," Lafayette wrote. "I seem to have had an anticipation of our future friendship, and what I have done out of esteem and respect for your excellency's name and reputation, I should do now out of mere love for General Washington himself."[13] Lafayette left Albany for Valley Forge on March 31, 1778.

⊞

Two months prior, Benjamin Franklin, Silas Deane, and their colleague Arthur Lee had successfully concluded a Treaty of Alliance with France. The treaty, which the parties signed on February 6, 1778, created a formal military alliance between the two nations. France and the United States pledged that neither would agree to a separate "truce or peace" with Great Britain and that American independence would be a condition of any future peace agreement.[14]

Word did not reach the United States about the potentially tide-turning alliance until after Lafayette had arrived back at Valley Forge late in April. On March 17, four days after France officially informed the British about the treaty, England declared war on France. The American military leaders immediately realized the import of the formal alliance with France. "I have mentioned the matter to such Officers as I have seen, and I believe no event was ever received with a more heart felt joy," George Washington wrote in a May 1 letter to Congress.[15]

A few days later, after Congress ratified the treaty, Washington issued a general order, telling the troops: "Upon a signal given, the whole Army will Huzza! 'Long Live the King of France.'"[16] And on May 6, Continental Army troops lined up at Valley Forge, 10,000 men strong. They shouted their huzzahs after each of three thirteen-cannon salutes, cheered King Louis XVI and the American states, and then each man fired his musket in turn, creating what was known as a running fire.

⊞

One consequence of the new Franco-American treaty and England's declaration of war against France was England's decision to widen its war in the Americas by attacking French possessions in the Caribbean. To do so, Sir George Germain, Britain's London-based secretary of state for the colonies, ordered General Henry Clinton—who was about to take over the war effort from Howe—to move 5,000 troops from North America to the Caribbean and to move 3,000 men to Florida to ward off a potential Spanish threat. The strategy also called for taking all British troops out of Philadelphia and occupying New York City and Rhode Island, leaving only defensive units in Canada. Finally, the British would seek to influence the Southern states of North Carolina, South Carolina, and Georgia (significant Loyalist strongholds) to detach themselves from the Revolution.

On May 18, Washington sent Lafayette out with some 2,000 men to try to find out where the British were going—the expedition that resulted in Lafayette's narrow and brilliant escape from the British at Barren Hill in Philadelphia.

❖

On June 18, 1778, the British finished their evacuation of Philadelphia. General Clinton marched his 10,000 British and Hessian troops, along with their baggage, cannons, and some Loyalists, across the Delaware River into New Jersey on their way to New York City. Some 3,000 other Philadelphia Loyalists, who had celebrated during the nearly nine-month British occupation, also left the city, sailing on ships up the Delaware to arrive eventually in New York. Within days, Washington and his Continental Army troops reentered the city, and he turned Philadelphia over to its newly appointed military governor, General Benedict Arnold.

When the Continental Congress adjourned on June 27 in York, the next order of business was to move the nation's capital back to Philadelphia. On July 2, 1778, Congress returned to Philadelphia, nearly two years after the adoption of the Declaration of Independence in that city.

CHAPTER 5

Cannon Fire Was Exchanged
All Day

The young Frenchman moves toward the enemy in raptures with
his command and burning to distinguish himself.

—Dr. James McHenry, June 25, 1778[1]

AFTER SKILLFULLY AND BRAVELY EXTRICATING HIMSELF AND HIS MEN
from the British trap at Barren Hill, the Marquis de Lafayette's stock
rose even higher with his mentor, George Washington. So much so
that in June 1778, Washington decided to have Lafayette play a
leading role in an operation that led to the Battle of Monmouth
Court House in New Jersey: the Revolutionary War battle with the
second-largest number of ground forces (more than 20,000). It was
also the longest battle in terms of constant action and was the last

big engagement in the Northern states between the Continental Army and the British.

Washington expected that the new French alliance would turn the tide against the British. The first dividend would be the imminent arrival of an eleven-ship squadron of French navy ships carrying some 4,000 marines that had set sail on April 13 from Toulon under Vice Admiral Charles-Henri Théodat, the Comte d'Estaing. With that in mind, Washington met with his Council of War at Valley Forge on June 17 to decide what to do about British General Henry Clinton's 10,000 men who were slowly marching northward in central New Jersey en route to New York.

The council could not agree on how to proceed. No one argued for a full-scale assault on the British. However, several generals—including Brigadier General Anthony Wayne, Alexander Hamilton, Nathanael Greene, and Lafayette—pushed hard to attack at least one part of the British line of troops. As Lafayette put it: "It would be disgraceful for the leaders, and humiliating for the troops, to allow the enemy to traverse the Jerseys with impunity."[2]

Lafayette wanted to attack Clinton's rear guard, saying "it was necessary to follow the British, to maneuver carefully, to profit from any separation of forces and in short to seize the most favorable opportunities and positions."[3]

Washington's second in command, Charles Lee, the cantankerous forty-seven-year-old British-born major general, argued against any kind of aggressive move. Lee, who had been held prisoner by the British from December 1776 to March 1778, argued that the Americans should confine themselves to a series of harassing guerrilla attacks on Clinton's men.

Washington did not make his decision then but did send out some troops to join New Jersey militia elements to follow and hound Clinton by destroying bridges, cutting down trees to block roads, filling wells with stones and poisoning others, as well as laying ambushes with hit-and-run sharpshooters. Following a second Council of War on June 24 at Hopewell, New Jersey, Washington went for the more aggressive approach, urged on once more by the ever-assertive young French general.

"I would lay my fortune, all that I possess in the world, that if [a detachment of 2,000 to 2,500 men] is sent in the proper time," Lafayette wrote to Washington that day, "some good effect, and no harm, shall arise of it."[4]

The next day, Washington moved his troops north and east to Kingston, New Jersey, just outside of Princeton. He ordered Lafayette to take charge of some 4,200 men—3,000 Continentals and about 1,200 militiamen, about half of his force—and to go after Clinton's rear guard, which was marching toward the small village of Monmouth Court House. "You are to use the most effectual means for gaining the enemy's left flank and rear," Washington's order said, "and giving them every degree of annoyance."[5]

Washington sent Alexander Hamilton to be Lafayette's second in command. Lee, at first, went along with allowing Lafayette to lead the fight. The order suited Lafayette just fine. But that same day, June 25, 1778, Lee changed his mind and decided that he wanted to take charge of Washington's army against the British. He first approached Lafayette. "I place my fortune and my honor in your hands," Lafayette quoted Lee as saying. "You are too generous to make me lose either of them."[6] Lafayette said he would accept the change and sent word to Washington.

Lee then wrote to Washington, speaking condescendingly of "the Young Volunteering General," and arguing that he, Lee, was more suited to lead the detachment because he was Washington's second in command. If Lafayette stayed in command, Lee told Washington, "both myself and Lord Sterlin [General William Alexander, known as Lord Stirling] will be disgrac'd."[7] Washington gave in. He sent Lafayette the bad news the next day:

> General Lee's uneasiness [over Washington naming Lafayette to command the troops was] rather increasing than abating, and your

politeness in wishing to ease him of it has induced me to detach him from this Army, with a part of it, to reinforce, or at least cover, the several detachments under your command, at present.

At the same time that I felt for Genl. Lee's distress of mind, I have had an eye to your wishes, and the delicacy of your situation; and have, therefore, obtained a promise from him, that when he gives you notice of his approach and command, he will request you to prosecute any plan you may have already concerted for the purpose of attacking or otherwise annoying the Enemy.[8]

◈

Two days later, on June 27, Lee caught up with Clinton at Monmouth Court House. Washington gave the word to attack the British left flank. But Lee dithered and then did little more than tell his men to be ready for action sometime soon. The following day, June 28, Lee's troops met the rear of the British and Hessian army a few miles north of Monmouth Court House. The battle began with skirmishing. Lee reacted by issuing a series of conflicting orders that did little more than confuse his subordinates, Lafayette included. Then Lee himself became bewildered and couldn't decide if the British were getting ready to retreat or attack.

He finally ordered Lafayette and his other commanders to assault the British rear guard from the left and right, and for Anthony Wayne to feign an attack. But Lee never adequately conveyed those orders to Wayne and the other commanding officers. Lee instructed Lafayette to cross an open field and hit the British on the left. Lafayette obeyed, but his position quickly became too precarious, and he moved to a better one. This left the other divisions out in the open, and they were forced to retreat.

While confusion reigned on the American side, Clinton realized what was happening and ordered General Wilhelm von Knyphausen to cover the left flank and move out. Clinton also dispatched Lieutenant General Charles Cornwallis (with fourteen battalions and the

Fourteenth Light Dragoons), perhaps Britain's most aggressive general, to face off against Lee's troops head-on. Clinton's tactics worked.

After Lee's attack on the British rear guard failed, the British began a furious fusillade against the exposed Americans. Lee lost control of the situation, and his troops retreated—pursued by Clinton's infantry. The rout was on. Lee stood by helplessly as his men ran from the battle. Lafayette, in desperation, sent for Washington, who had asked Lee earlier for a situation report and had received word from him that things were under control.

Washington wisely didn't believe Lee, and as he moved toward the fighting, he saw the evidence of Lee's misinformation: American troops on the run from the British. The retreating men said that Lee had ordered them to fall back. Washington then came face-to-face with Lee, and they argued. Washington sent Lee to the rear and rallied the retreating masses into a blocking force with Lafayette at his side.

Washington performed fearlessly and heroically from atop his white charger. The men responded and regrouped and held the British before making an organized retreat to form a stronger defensive line.

"I never saw the general to so much advantage," Alexander Hamilton later wrote. "His coolness and firmness were admirable. He instantly took maneuvers for checking the enemy's advance and giving time for the army, which was very near, to form and make a proper disposition."[9]

Washington brought his artillery up on his right under Greene, with Stirling on his left and Lafayette in charge of a second line of about 800 men armed with cannons on a rise. The battle then picked up in intensity. Washington led a charge, and the two sides had at each other in one of the fiercest battles and artillery duels of the Revolutionary War. Cannon fire went back and forth all day, and twice the British seemed to break through the American lines.

But by midday, after hours of fighting in intense heat, including hand-to-hand combat, the Redcoats wilted and Cornwallis gave up the fight. Then Washington launched a counterattack, and by mid-afternoon the rest of the British withdrew. Washington considered pursuing them, but his men also were exhausted.

"The heat was so intense that soldiers fell dead without having been touched, and the battlefield soon became untenable," Lafayette wrote, with perhaps at least some exaggeration, although the temperature may have hit 100 degrees and the humidity was intense.[10]

Lafayette fought well and hard at Monmouth Court House. "The young Frenchman...moves toward the enemy...in raptures with his command and burning to distinguish himself," the Irish-born surgeon Dr. James McHenry, then on Washington's staff, wrote in his diary during the battle.[11] But the marquis played down his role in the fighting in his memoirs; although he noted that he had fought on an empty stomach and kept changing assignments from 4:00 A.M. until nightfall.

After sundown, Clinton allowed his men to rest and then woke them at around 10:00 P.M. The British, leaving their campfires burning, marched north at around midnight toward Sandy Hook on the extreme northern tip of the Jersey Shore. It was just a short boat ride from there into New York Harbor across Lower New York Bay and into Manhattan. Washington did not follow Clinton into that British stronghold but decided to take his army to meet up with other Continental troops camped along the Hudson River.

❖

Who won the Battle of Monmouth Court House? The British held off the Americans and escaped with relatively few casualties. But the Americans, after Lee's missteps, counted many small victories from the battle. The troops, for one thing, generally fought well. The training under General Friedrich Wilhelm von Steuben—and to a lesser but not insignificant degree under Lafayette—paid off as the Continental soldiers for the first time showed battlefield discipline and acumen with their bayonets, muskets, and rifles.

Although the British managed to retreat, their casualties were higher than the Americans'. Washington reported burying 4 British officers and 245 privates, and noted a "considerable" number of enemy wounded.[12] Other reports had some 600 British and Hessian troops missing. The official tally on the American side was 69 killed, 37 dead of heat stroke, and 161 wounded. Also to the Americans' advantage was the fact that the British had abandoned Philadelphia and New Jersey, giving the Americans a big morale boost.

✦

The Marquis de Lafayette joined his American comrades to celebrate the second birthday of the United States on July 4, 1778, at Brunswick (now New Brunswick), New Jersey. It was a big celebration, complete with gun salutes and extra rations of rum for the men. That same day, Clinton sailed with his army from Sandy Hook to the safety of Manhattan Island.

July 4 also brought more big news: the Comte d'Estaing—who, like Lafayette, was born in Auvergne and who was related to him by marriage—had arrived off the Eastern Shore of Virginia with a fleet of twelve ships of the line, four frigates, and some 4,000 French marines. Now for the first time, Washington would have naval forces to compete with those of his enemy—not to mention marines, who would soon become the first French body of fighting men to participate directly in the war.

Washington opted—with the full support of Lafayette—to deploy the French fleet to the north. There they would join with Major General John Sullivan's 3,000-man Continental Army force and 6,000 Boston militiamen under the command of Major General John Hancock, who had recently resigned as president of the Continental

Congress and returned to his home state. The idea was to deal a punishing blow to the British in New England by ousting their 6,000-man force from Newport, Rhode Island.

Washington decided that Lafayette would play an important role in the fighting in Rhode Island. Washington gave him 2,000 men—the First Rhode Island Brigade under Brigadier General James Varnum, the Second Massachusetts Brigade under Brigadier General John Glover, and a detachment of troops under Colonel Henry Jackson of Massachusetts. On July 22, Washington ordered Lafayette to "march them with all convenient expedition and by the best Routs" to Providence, Rhode Island, and rendezvous with Sullivan.[13]

Washington also named Lafayette field commander of all the American forces on this crucial mission—second in command, that is, to Sullivan, with whom the young Frenchman had fought closely at the Battle of Brandywine. Another advantage for giving the twenty-year-old such a big role: he was Washington's only commander who could speak both French and English well. The Comte d'Estaing did not speak English at all. Lafayette was overjoyed. The major general further rejoiced after word came from d'Estaing that he wanted Lafayette to take joint command of the French marines and his American troops for the anticipated showdown with the British.

Everything seemed to be in place for a potential war-changing operation. The plan was to make a two-pronged attack on Newport, which is on Aquidneck Island in Narragansett Bay. D'Estaing's fleet would sail in and hit the British from the south side of the island, and Sullivan's men would mount an assault from the north. When d'Estaing's fleet arrived off Newport on July 29, he and Sullivan communicated using intermediaries. From that point on, nearly everything went downhill for the Americans and French.

D'Estaing, for one thing, was not in the best of moods. The long voyage from France had taken a severe toll on his marines, many of whom died at sea of malnutrition and scurvy. D'Estaing was still unhappy, too, about his first aborted mission—on July 9 when he had arrived off Sandy Hook and found that the water was too shallow for him to navigate an attack on the British fleet. Then, when he made it to the coast of Rhode Island, d'Estaing learned to his great dismay that the sea lanes in Narragansett Bay were extremely narrow and very difficult to maneuver. Any engagement close to Newport would be difficult, at best.

To make matters worse, he and Sullivan did not get along. The gruff New Englander had no love for France, and much less for French aristocrats such as the Comte d'Estaing. The language barrier didn't help matters either.

Lafayette and his men arrived in Providence on August 2. His first order of business was to meet with d'Estaing, which he did aboard the comte's flagship, *Le Languedoc*. But Lafayette found d'Estaing difficult to deal with at first. D'Estaing was not pleased that the young Frenchman had blatantly disregarded the orders of King Louis XVI when he made his escape from France the previous year. Lafayette responded that he regretted his actions and that his mission now was to serve the king by fighting the English.

Lafayette won the argument. "No one is in a better position than this young general officer," d'Estaing wrote to the French naval minister, "to become an additional bond of unity between France and America."[14]

D'Estaing also reiterated his idea that Lafayette take the French marines into his command. "I confess I feel very happy to think of my cooperating with them," Lafayette later wrote to Washington, "and had I contriv'd in my mind an agreeable dream, I could not have wish'd a more pleasing event than my joining my countrymen with my brothers of America under my command and the same standards. When I left Europe I was very far from hoping for such an agreeable turn of our business in the American glorious revolution."[15]

Lafayette tried to make peace between d'Estaing and Sullivan as he shuttled back and forth from *Le Languedoc* to shore to relay messages between the two men. He talked Sullivan into providing food supplies to d'Estaing's all-but-starving sailors and marines. This mollified d'Estaing, at least for the time being.

Sullivan and d'Estaing eventually agreed that the French admiral would take his men to the northern end of Aquidneck Island and march south toward Newport, where d'Estaing would send in his marines. But Sullivan then learned that the commander of the British Rhode Island garrison, the veteran fighter Major General Robert Pigot, had moved his forces back toward the city. Therefore, Sullivan quickly brought his troops in to take over the northern part of the island. This did not go over well with d'Estaing and his officers, who reacted angrily to the abrupt change of plans. Any rapprochement between Sullivan and the French ended. Then came word that Admiral Richard Howe and a squadron of British warships were heading up from New York to take on d'Estaing.

On August 10, d'Estaing moved his fleet into open water to face off against Howe. But the next day, before the would-be epic naval battle began, they were suddenly hit by a vicious storm with fierce gales. It raged for nearly three days and caused so much damage to both fleets that the fight never happened. After the howling winds died down, the British sailed back to New York, and d'Estaing limped back to Narragansett Bay, arriving on August 20.

Sullivan, in the interim, had moved his men southward toward Newport to battle Pigot, and he expected d'Estaing to support him from the sea. That assistance did not come. What's more, d'Estaing changed his mind again and decided that Lafayette would not command a combined French-American force at Newport. That day, Lafayette and Nathanael Greene met with d'Estaing aboard *Le Languedoc* "both to gain some time and to propose either an attack in force or the stationing of ships in the Providence River," as Lafayette put it.[16]

D'Estaing did nothing to further French-American relations by turning down that request and immediately sailing to Boston for repairs, rather than supporting Sullivan against the British there in Newport. "When the vessels departed," Lafayette wrote in his memoirs, "there was a general feeling of distress and indignation."[17] Sullivan, Lafayette said, "was carried away by his anger and added to the orders of the day [of August 24] the statement that 'our allies have abandoned us.'"[18] Sullivan had another reason to be unhappy: he had lost a significant number of his own men, many of whom deserted, and only had about 5,000 able-bodied troops at his command.

After hearing from Congress, which admonished him for his behavior, Sullivan sent Lafayette to Boston to make amends with d'Estaing and try to convince John Hancock to help refit the French fleet. Sullivan put his faith in the ability of the twenty-year-old Frenchman to be a force of reason in mediating with d'Estaing—a vivid illustration of Lafayette's rapid maturation and increasing ability to rein in his youthful enthusiasm and use his wits and personality for the good of the American cause.

Lafayette arrived in the city after a furious, seven-hour horseback ride to meet with Hancock. The former Boston shipbuilder threw a lavish dinner in Beacon Hill for d'Estaing, after which Hancock presented the French count with a portrait of George Washington. "I never saw a man so glad of possessing his sweet heart's picture, as the admiral was to receive yours," Lafayette later wrote to Washington.[19]

The next day, August 30, Lafayette rode back to Rhode Island, where he found Sullivan's men in retreat on the northwest end of Aquidneck Island. Greene and Sullivan, outnumbered almost four to one and without naval support, had engaged Pigot the day before. The Americans, with the help of a battalion of Rhode Island African American soldiers made up of former slaves and freedmen, held off a furious land and sea assault by the British and Hessians that lasted into the night.

When Lafayette arrived, the Americans were retreating. He immediately took command of the rear guard and helped in the final evacuation of American troops from Newport by boat. Lafayette reportedly was the last man off the island.

After lamenting in a letter to Washington two days later that he was "once more depriv'd of my fighting expectations," Lafayette praised Sullivan's leadership and painted the engagement in positive colors. The "action does great honor to Gal. Sullivan," he said. "He retreated in good order, he oppos'd very properly every effort of the enemy, he never sent troops but well supported, and display'd a great coolness during the whole day."[20]

The evacuation of Newport, Lafayette opined, was "extremely well perform'd, and my *private opinion* is that if both events are satisfactory to us, they are very shameful for the British generals and troops. They had indeed fine chances as to cut us to pieces."[21]

The Continental Congress passed a resolution praising Sullivan, Lafayette, and the men for their bravery. When he learned of the resolution, Lafayette wrote a heartfelt thank-you letter to President of Congress Henry Laurens, saying: "The moment I heard of America, I lov'd her. The moment I knew she was fighting for freedom, I burnt with the desire of bleeding for her—and the moment I shall be able of serving her in any time or any part of the world, will be among the happiest ones in my life."[22]

❖

Each side suffered about 250 deaths in the Battle of Rhode Island, after which most of Lafayette's men went home for the winter. General George Washington made for his winter quarters in upstate New York near West Point. Lafayette set up for the winter in Bristol, Rhode Island. As for d'Estaing, after his fleet was repaired in Boston, he sailed to the West Indies early in November. Without the support of the French fleet, the once-promising French-American alliance seemed to be, at the very least, in a tenuous position.

CHAPTER 6

An Uncommon Maturity of Judgment

I love the trade of war passionately.

—Marquis de Lafayette, June 10, 1779[1]

As Lafayette set up winter quarters in Bristol, Rhode Island, on September 1, 1778, he had two basic but conflicting things on his mind. First, he wanted to go home to France to see his wife and family and to take up arms against the British under the French flag. On the other hand, he also was itching to take part in a joint French-American invasion of Canada—an assault in which he envisioned playing an integral role. When Lafayette heard that week that the British were preparing to leave New York and disperse their troops to the West Indies; Halifax, Nova Scotia; and other parts of Canada, he saw his opportunity to step up the pressure for his Canada-invasion plan.

Lafayette had been peppering General George Washington, the Continental Congress, and Vice Admiral Charles-Henri Théodat— the Comte d'Estaing—with letters pushing for the invasion. The marquis kept up the written assault with a missive to Washington on September 7 (the day after his 21st birthday), saying he very much hoped that Canada "will be your occupation next winter and spring." That thought, he said, "alters a plan I had to make a voyage home some months hence, however, as long as you fight I want to fight along with you, and I much desire to see your excellency in Quebec next summer."[2]

The next day, September 8, Lafayette wrote to d'Estaing expressing his "impatience to see the French strike some blow" in North America. Lafayette went on to tell d'Estaing that he was consumed with thoughts of "of being reunited with you, of Halifax surrendering, of St. Augustine [Florida] taken, of the British West Indies in flames, and of all acknowledging that nothing can resist the French."[3]

A few days later, Lafayette heard from his father-in-law in France for the first time since he had arrived in North America. The Duc d'Ayen advised Lafayette, who had been all but begging to come home and join the French Army and fight the British, to stay put. The reason, he said, was that there would be no fighting against the British on the Continent.

Hearing from the duke left Lafayette "enchanted and overjoyed," he said in a long, fulsome letter to his father-in-law on September 11. "I now rejoice that I have [stayed in the United States]," Lafayette wrote. "The arrival of the French fleet upon this coast has offered me the agreeable prospect of acting in concert with it, and of being a happy spectator of the glory of the French banner." He said that even after the near debacle at Newport, he had "not lost the sanguine hopes of the future, which the great talents of M. d'Estaing have inspired us with."[4] Two days later, Lafayette wrote a lengthy, passionate letter to his wife, Adrienne, saying how much he missed her and expressing the fervent hope that he would be sailing home soon.

Lafayette's lobbying to invade Canada came to nothing. Washington would not sanction this expedition and told Lafayette so several times. An incursion just would not work logistically or strategically with Washington's troops hunkered down safely in winter quarters arrayed around New York, he argued—not to mention the fact that winter was coming on. On September 25, Washington wrote to Lafayette, advising him to go to France that winter rather than stay in North America hoping to take part in an invasion of Canada. First, he wrote, the British would have had to "withdraw wholly, or in part from their present posts, to leave us at liberty to detach largely from this Army." Second, the logistics of waging war in Canada during winter would be especially daunting because of the cold and the difficulties of attaining food and other supplies.[5]

Lafayette did not argue with Washington, but he also did not abandon his lobbying or his fierce anti-British feelings. He continued to write to d'Estaing, Congress, Washington, and others proposing military action against the British in Bermuda, the West Indies, Newfoundland, Florida, New York, and Georgia. The marquis decided he could best push for his plan by returning to France and making his case in person at the French court. Lafayette soon asked Washington for permission to take a winter furlough to go home. He said he wanted to do so to fight the English, stressing that he would have stayed in this country if the Canada offensive—or any other move against the British—were in the offing. Washington agreed.

Washington expressed his thoughts on the matter in an October 6 letter to the Continental Congress in which he stressed that Lafayette was still devoted to the American cause. Washington mentioned his "reluctance to part with an Officer who unites all the military fire of youth" and "an uncommon maturity of judgment" but said he would go along with the request provided it was only a furlough.[6]

On October 13, 1778, Lafayette, who by then had left New England and returned to Philadelphia, wrote to Congress formally requesting leave from the Continental Army. Congress granted the furlough request on October 21 and instructed the president of Congress, Henry Laurens, to write a formal thank-you letter to Lafayette for his services, which he did three days later. Congress also decided to honor Lafayette with a sword, which it ordered to be made in Paris to be presented to Lafayette by the American minister when he arrived home. Lastly, Congress wrote a letter to King Louis XVI singing Lafayette's praises.

On October 27, Lafayette left Philadelphia on his way to Boston, where he would sail for France. He rode all day and into many nights in nearly constant rain and to much attention along the road from American citizens. Wherever he stopped, Lafayette was wined and dined, and he indulged heartily. When he arrived at Fishkill, New York, not far from Washington's camp, on November 2, the young marquis fell seriously ill with a high fever accompanied by an intense headache. Washington came to his bedside; he also sent his personal physician, Dr. John Cochran, to attend the Frenchman. It took Lafayette nearly a month to recover from what he called a "very severe and dangerous fitt of illness."[7]

Dr. James Thacher, a physician from Massachusetts serving with the First Virginia Regiment, visited Lafayette at Fishkill on November 27 and found him "just recovering from a fever...in his chair of convalescence." The twenty-four-year-old Thacher described Lafayette as "nearly six feet high, large but not corpulent, being not more than twenty-one years of age. He is not very elegant in his form, his shoulders being broad and high, nor is there a perfect symmetry in his features, his forehead is remarkably high, his nose large and long, eyebrows prominent and projecting over a fine animated hazel eye."[8]

Lafayette's "countenance," Thacher noted, "is interesting and impressive. He converses in broken English, and displays the manners and address of an accomplished gentleman. Considering him a French nobleman of distinguished character, and a great favorite of General Washington, I felt myself highly honored by this interview."[9]

During the first of week of December 1778, Lafayette had recovered sufficiently to ride to Boston, accompanied by Washington's physician, where the Frenchman continued to lobby for a Canadian invasion.[10] Congress finally put an end to the issue on January 3, 1779, when its new president, John Jay, wrote to Lafayette in Boston telling him directly that Congress had decided there would be no invasion of America's northern neighbor. The American war effort, Jay said, "should be employed in expelling the enemy from her own shores, before the liberation of a neighbouring province is undertaken."[11]

On January 5, two days after Jay wrote that letter (which Lafayette would not receive until May), Lafayette boarded the aptly named *Alliance,* a new American frigate that Congress put at his disposal, at Boston Harbor. He carried a letter Washington had written on December 28 from Philadelphia addressed to Benjamin Franklin. After working behind the scenes on America's behalf at the French court since 1777, Franklin had become minister plenipotentiary to France on September 14, 1778—the first American minister (ambassador) to the court of Versailles.

In the letter, Washington effusively praised Lafayette, describing his "gallantry" at the Battle of Brandywine, his "success" at

Barren Hill, the "brilliant retreat" he orchestrated at Monmouth Court House, and his "services" on Rhode Island. Those actions, Washington said, "are such proofs of his zeal, military ardour and talents as have endeared him to America, and must greatly recommend him to his Prince."[12]

Washington told Franklin that he had "a very particular friendship for" Lafayette and asked the American minister to help the young man with "whatever services you may have it in your power to render him."[13]

❖

The *Alliance* set sail on January 11, 1779. The journey took nearly four weeks, the frigate arriving at Brest on February 6. A few days later, Lafayette, wearing his American military uniform, arrived by coach at Versailles where he met with Foreign Minister Comte de Vergennes and Prime Minister Comte de Maurepas. France had officially been in a state of war with England since the previous July. But except for an exchange of fire between warships off the Brittany coast, there had not been any actual fighting. Lafayette burned with desire to push France into action. But before he could state his case, he was arrested.

The arrest was a face-saving slap on the wrist by King Louis XVI because Lafayette had not been officially reprimanded for having disobeyed the royal order not to leave France two years earlier. The warrant confined Lafayette to eight days of house arrest—in the extremely un-prison-like Noailles family mansion, where he reunited with his wife and young daughter. Lafayette wrote a nominal letter of apology to the king, and when the sentence ended, the young general burst onto the Parisian social scene.

Dubbed the "hero of two worlds," Lafayette was feted both at the court of King Louis XVI and by the people of Paris. He soon became the biggest celebrity in the country. The king invited him to join his hunting parties. The young marquis received wild ovations when he and Adrienne appeared at such public venues as theaters and operas. As Lafayette put it, immodestly yet accurately, in his memoirs: "I enjoyed both favour at the court of Versailles, and popularity at Paris. I was the theme of conversation in every circle."[14]

On March 3, Lafayette became a lieutenant commander (a *mestre de camp,* or cavalry colonel) with his own regiment in the King's Dragoons—a promotion that cost him the huge sum of 80,000 livres. He was now an officer in both the United States and the French Armies.

In those capacities, he met often with Maurepas, Vergennes, and the king's other ministers. Lafayette also frequently conferred with the colorful Franklin, with whom he soon grew very close, and with John Adams, who had joined Franklin as an American commissioner in April 1778. Lafayette used his high connections and his celebrity to work tirelessly in promoting his two missions in life: continued French support for the American Revolution (which was going very badly after the disastrous fall of Savannah, Georgia, late in December 1778) and plans for a full-scale French military assault against England.

✠

Throughout the month of March 1779, Lafayette pushed hard for a raid on the coasts of England and Ireland, then under English rule. He found an ally in John Paul Jones, the Scottish-born American Navy captain who had been working for the American commissioners in Paris since he had sailed his sloop *Ranger* to France in December 1777. In April and May of the previous year, Jones had made a series of raids along the Irish and Scottish coasts, capturing an English naval sloop.

In March 1779, Jones, in command of a former French ship he had renamed the *Bonhomme Richard,* was anxious to return to the fray. Soon he, Lafayette, Franklin, and several French ministers devised a plan to invade England with Jones leading the naval contingent and Lafayette commanding some 1,200 ground troops.

When that plan never came to fruition, Lafayette turned his lobbying efforts to backing a joint French-Spanish expedition against England. That, too, seemed to come to nothing, when on May 22, Lafayette received orders to take command of his King's Dragoon regiment in Saintes in the southwest of France. Lafayette obeyed the order, but unhappily, because he believed that Vergennes and Maurepas had given up invading England.

But the French and Spanish had not abandoned the idea of invading. Lafayette and his regiment, he soon found out, were scheduled to be part of a newly planned invasion made up of some 20,000 French troops that would land at the Isle of Wight and Portsmouth supported by the combined French and Spanish fleets. When Lafayette learned of this plan, he gleefully began drilling his troops in preparation for what promised to be a massive engagement.

"Don't forget that I love the trade of war passionately," Lafayette wrote to Vergennes on June 10, "that I consider myself born especially to play that game, that I have been spoiled for two years by the habit of having been in command and of winning great confidence." He then suggested that it wouldn't be a bad idea if he would "be the first to reach [England] and the first to plant the French flag in the heart of that insolent nation."[15]

On June 13, 1779, Lafayette received orders to report at Versailles to the Comte de Vaux, who would be leading the invasion out of Le Havre. Lafayette would be his *aide maréchal général des logis*— the general responsible for organizing marches and the quartering of troops.[16]

On June 16, Spain sent its official declaration of grievances to England, the equivalent of a declaration of war. Lafayette arrived at Le Havre on July 1. While waiting for the assault on England, he continued to lobby for France to widen its participation in the Revolutionary

War. Lafayette suggested in a July 18 letter to Vergennes, for example, that he should be the man to lead a 4,300-man French force to retake Rhode Island and move against the British in New York, Virginia, the Carolinas, Florida, and elsewhere—and then invade Canada.[17]

On July 23, the Spanish and French fleets rendezvoused off Cape Finisterre on the extreme northwest coast of Spain to get ready for the invasion. The huge combined fleet entered the English Channel in mid-August. Then just about everything went wrong.

During the next four weeks, smallpox ran rampant on the ships. Storms blew in. The British fleet's faster ships stayed just out of reach of French and Spanish ships' guns. On September 14, the French and Spanish called off the invasion, and the combined fleet sailed back to France. That bad news was followed for Lafayette by some good news: on December 24, Adrienne gave birth to a boy, Lafayette's first and only son. He named the child Georges Washington de Lafayette.

❖

After the Spanish and French officially abandoned the invasion, Lafayette turned his attention to returning to the fight in the United States—and to getting the French government to send more troops and ships to boost the American cause. He used his usual method of operation: a stream of letters and persistent personal visits to Vergennes and Maurepas, as well as to Washington, Franklin, and other influential Americans.

Lafayette also worked closely and successfully along with Franklin to get Vergennes and Maurepas to provide significant amounts of arms and munitions to the Americans. Then, on March 5, 1780, within days after Lafayette had met with King Louis XVI wearing his American uniform, the official word came from Vergennes. Lafayette was to "hasten to join" Washington in America and be the bearer of very good news: the king would send six ships of the line and 6,000 "regular infantry troops at the onset of spring."[18]

Lafayette, though, would not be in charge of the mission. Vergennes instead chose the Comte de Rochambeau, a fifty-four-year-old veteran general, to command the French ground troops. The Chevalier de Ternay would lead Rochambeau's French naval escort fleet. Lafayette, by all accounts (including his own), readily accepted the decision. He was simply happy to be going back to America, ahead of a huge influx of French troops and ships, and—no doubt—to be heading back into the fighting that he all but loved.

The acceptance of Rochambeau was another example of Lafayette's maturity and his growing leadership skills. He readily acceded to Vergennes' decision to promote Rochambeau even though he would have loved to be in charge of the French troops. Lafayette suppressed his own ego for the good of the cause—and knowing that even though he wouldn't be leading the French troops, he still would be playing a prominent role in the war.

❖

After a farewell visit (again in his American uniform) to King Louis XVI, Lafayette said his goodbyes to Franklin and went to Versailles, where he worked out the final arrangements for the order of battle once Rochambeau arrived in the United States. The French general would take orders from Washington, although the American commander in chief would consult Rochambeau on all matters of strategy. And Lafayette and the other Frenchmen fighting in the Continental Army would remain under Washington's command.

Vergennes issued Lafayette his final instructions on March 5. He was to go to America, immediately join Washington, and inform him in confidence of the king's commitment of ships and troops.

The French military contingent, Vergennes said, echoing the agreement he had worked out with Lafayette, "will be purely auxiliary, and in this capacity, it will act only under General Washington's orders." Rochambeau would take orders from Washington "for everything that does not relate to the internal regulation of his corps." And Ternay would "support with all his power all operations in which his cooperation is required."[19]

On March 9, 1780, Lafayette arrived at the southwestern French seaport town of Rochefort. Four days later, on March 13, he set sail for America aboard the French frigate *L'Hermione*. The journey back to America started out inauspiciously. Two days out, high winds ripped off the mainmast, and the ship limped back to port, chased by three English warships. *L'Hermione* departed again on March 20 and arrived in Boston on April 27.

CHAPTER 7

A Decisive Moment

From this time until the termination of the campaign of 1781, . . . his service was of incessant activity, always signalized by military talents unsurpassed, and by a spirit never to be subdued.

—John Quincy Adams, December 31, 1834[1]

THE MARQUIS DE LAFAYETTE WAS MORE THAN READY TO RE-ENTER THE fray after a thirty-eight-day sea journey. Before the *Hermione* even made shore—as the ship entered Boston Harbor—Lafayette wrote to General George Washington, telling his surrogate father of "the joy" he felt "in finding myself again one of your loving soldiers." The twenty-two-year-old hero of two worlds was itching to deliver Foreign Minister Comte de Vergennes' orders to Washington—"affairs of utmost importance," he told his beloved commander in chief, "which

I should at first communicate to you alone." Said orders, Lafayette said portentously, would bring "a great public good."[2]

Washington and the American cause desperately needed good news. It was April 1780, and the Continental Army had suffered greatly during the winter of 1779–1780, an extraordinarily bitter one that nearly dealt a death blow to Washington's underpaid, underclothed, underfed, and undersupplied troops.

"The oldest people now living in this country do not remember so hard a winter as the one we are now emerging from," Washington had written to Lafayette on March 18. "In a word, the severity of the frost exceeded anything of the kind that had ever been experienced in this climate before."[3]

Johan de Kalb spoke of the "uninterrupted and unvarying cold of the winter," in which snowdrifts grew twelve feet high, ice in the rivers was six feet thick, and temperatures sunk so low in February that the ink froze in his pen. "Those who have only been in Valley Forge or Middlebrook during the last two winters but have not tasted the cruelties of this one, know not what it is to suffer," Kalb wrote. "The times are growing worse from hour to hour."[4]

The bitterly cold weather exacerbated the Continental Army's other serious problems. The quartermaster corps barely functioned, Loyalists would not sell food or supplies to the troops, and many Americans sympathetic to the cause would not extend credit to the army because they were not likely to be repaid. What's more, deep divisions in the Continental Congress, which did not have the power to tax or supply the troops directly, led to a near legislative gridlock. The state governments, moreover, which did have taxing and supply powers, often disagreed sharply with the national government and very often did not accede to congressional requests to feed and clothe the troops. Adding to the supply problem were the issues of the English shipping blockade, the American boycott of English goods, and the inevitable rise of domestic war profiteers.

Congress, acting as a federal government, and the very independent thirteen states all printed their own paper currencies. By the winter of 1779–1780, the nation and all the states found themselves deeply in debt. Congress alone owed tens of millions of dollars. The combination of these factors led to rampant inflation, and during the harsh winter of 1779–1780, the Continental dollar was nearly worthless.

"The dearth of necessaries of life is almost incredible, and increases from day to day," Kalb said at the time. "A hat costs four hundred dollars, a pair of boots the same, and everything else in proportion. The other day I was disposed to buy a pretty good horse. A price was asked which my pay for ten years would not have covered." Money, he said, "scatters like chaff before the wind, and expenses almost double from one day to the next, while income, of course, remains stationary."[5]

The upshot for Washington's reeling army was a severe shortage of food and the necessities of life: shoes, socks, tents, blankets, horses, and wagons. That led to increasing restlessness among the troops, the plummeting of morale, and not infrequent cases of desertion and outright mutinies.

After barely surviving the winter, Washington's army suffered a series of serious military setbacks, beginning with the fall of Charleston, South Carolina. On April 8, 1780, the British under Generals Henry Clinton and Charles Cornwallis surrounded Charleston by land and sea and then placed the city under a virtually airtight siege.

On May 12, the Americans under Major General Benjamin Lincoln surrendered. Lincoln waved the white flag with some 5,400 men under his command—by far the biggest mass surrender of the war. The British now had nearly complete control in South Carolina and Georgia, along with the support of many local Loyalists. Things only would get worse militarily for the Americans in the summer and fall of 1780.

❖

Back in Boston in late April 1780, Lafayette's arrival was the occasion for celebration, even though no one knew of the news he carried with him: the French military would soon be arriving on American shores. When word got out that Lafayette had returned, "every person ran to the shore; he was received with the loudest acclamations, and carried in triumph to the house of Governor Hancock, from whence he set out for head-quarters," Lafayette wrote. When Washington heard the young Frenchman had landed, Lafayette said, he reacted with "great emotion," and upon "receiving the despatch which announced to him this event, his eyes filled with tears of joy."[6]

Lafayette went to see Washington in Morristown, New Jersey, on May 10, where his surrogate father and commanding officer briefed him on the dire situation. Lafayette delivered the welcome news that the French expeditionary force—seven ships of the line, two frigates, several smaller armed vessels, and about 5,000 troops (about a thousand fewer than what Vergennes had promised)—was on its way.

Washington expressed the joy he felt at Lafayette's return and the imminent arrival of the French reinforcements in a May 13 letter to the Continental Congress. He sent the marquis to Philadelphia to deliver this most welcome news in person. Lafayette arrived two days later and met with the French minister (i.e., ambassador) to the United States, the Chevalier de La Luzerne, and then with members of Congress.

Lafayette received another warm greeting in the capital, then returned to Washington's headquarters to await the arrival of the French fleet. He went on to play a crucial role in coordinating the actions of the French and American Armies, including setting up a provisioning system for the French troops. This was not an easy task given the dismal performance of the Continental Army's quartermaster operation, which consistently had not been able to provide the army with sufficient supplies. Lafayette, moreover, would serve as Washington's primary liaison with the Comte de Rochambeau and Chevalier de Ternay—a plan La Luzerne and the Continental Congress endorsed.

❖

Lafayette also undertook another mission—a nonmilitary endeavor that would prove to be extremely valuable. He began lobbying the governors and other state officials to do their parts to provide men, materiel, and provisions to the American Army. On May 30, for example, Lafayette penned a long letter to Samuel Adams, an influential member of Congress from Massachusetts, whom he had met in Paris.

The war effort, Lafayette told Adams, was "particularly depending on the exertions of your State." He knew that "*Mr. Samuel Adams's influence* and popularity will be as heretofore employ'd to the salvation and glory of America."[7]

The next day Lafayette wrote to Pennsylvania Governor Joseph Reed, reporting that the Continental Army "is reduc'd to nothing," "wants provisions," and "has not one of the necessary means to make war." Unless the states provisioned the army and provided more troops, Lafayette told Reed, "we are lost."[8]

Lafayette wrote similar letters to other top officials, including Governors Jonathan Trumball of Connecticut and George Clinton of New York, and to the influential Massachusetts member of Congress, James Bowdoin. Within weeks, Lafayette's intense lobbying began paying dividends. Promises came in to Washington from several states to increase their contributions of troops, clothing, food, arms, and ammunition to the Continental Army. Moreover, Governor Reed's wife, Esther, organized a group of women in Philadelphia who raised a large amount of money to supply clothing to the army. Lafayette contributed a not-insignificant sum in the name of his wife. Other women's groups formed to work together to supply the army in other cities and states, as did associations of merchants and bankers. And significant numbers of militiamen signed up for the cause.

✦

Lafayette immersed himself in lobbying throughout the rest of the spring of 1780 and into the summer. Then came the news that the French fleet under Rochambeau was spotted off the coast near Boston. The ships entered Narragansett Bay on July 10. Rochambeau began landing his troops—three regiments (more than 3,000 men) under the command of the Marquis de Saint-Simon—two days later.

"This is a decisive moment; one of the most (I will go further and say the most) important America has seen," Washington had written in a May 28 letter to Reed.[9] Washington sent Lafayette to Newport, Rhode Island, to be his official liaison to Rochambeau and Ternay with a letter praising the young Frenchman. "As a General officer, I have the greatest confidence in him," Washington told the French officers. "As a friend, he is perfectly acquainted with my sentiments and opinions. He knows all the circumstances of our army and the country at large. All the information he gives, and all the positions he makes, I entreat you to consider as coming from me."[10]

The information at Newport, though, was not all good. For one thing, Rochambeau had about 5,000 marines and sailors—not the 6,000 or more the Americans were led to believe. The Americans also expected John Paul Jones to accompany the French fleet to harass British ships along the Atlantic Coast; he did not. What's more, about 2,000 of the French troops and as many as 1,300 sailors suffered from various debilitating illnesses and exhaustion after the long sea voyage and were not in fighting condition. Nor was the supply of arms, ammunition, and clothing what the Americans expected.

Rochambeau decided to wait for reinforcements in the form of an additional division of troops and more ships from France before he would take any offensive action. Then came reports that a British fleet under Admiral Thomas Graves, augmented by a squadron sent from England, had shown up off the Rhode Island coast and were getting ready to block the entrance to the harbor at Newport. Rochambeau responded by sending his ailing and healthy troops to occupy the recently vacated British works on Newport and by setting up his fleet in a defensive position offshore.

When Lafayette showed up on July 25, he was not happy. "I confess," he wrote to Washington on July 21, "it is impossible not to be very angry at Captain Jones' delay and much disappointed in our expectations."[11]

The ever-aggressive Lafayette, realizing that the shortage of troops, arms, and ammunition meant there would be no offensive operations for months—and probably not until 1781—dashed off intemperate letters to Rochambeau and Ternay complaining about the situation. The letters did not go over well.

Lafayette "proposes extravagant things to us," Rochambeau wrote to La Luzerne on August 14, "like taking Long Island and New York with a navy."[12] Rochambeau and Ternay decided they would not deal with Lafayette and would henceforth only communicate directly with Washington.

Lafayette wrote to Rochambeau and Ternay on August 18 apologizing for his unwise words. La Luzerne, the French ambassador, also came to the aid of his young countryman, using his diplomatic skills to convince Rochambeau that Lafayette spoke rashly only because he passionately cared about helping the Americans, and moreover, that Lafayette had Washington's full confidence.

Washington told Lafayette to be patient. Arms from the states, Washington said, "come in even slower than I expected; though we have still an abundance of fair promises and some earnest of performance from the Eastern states."[13]

❖

Given the French resolve to wait and the still-serious supply problems, Washington decided to bide his time and moved into a defensive posture in New York. On August 3, he appointed Benedict Arnold as commander at West Point. On August 16, Washington's army suffered one of its most costly defeats of the war at the Battle of Camden in South Carolina. Some 5,000 troops under Horatio Gates—who had pushed for and received command of the Southern Continental Army on July 26—were soundly defeated in a vicious fight that began at 2:00 A.M. The battle ended when Cornwallis vanquished Kalb's contingent of 600 Continental troops after Gates had fled with his men, who broke and ran after a British assault.

As many as 900 American troops perished at Camden and about 1,000 were taken prisoner in a battle that ended any hope of an American victory in the South. The crushing defeat ended Gates's short-lived tenure as commander of the Southern Army; Washington replaced him in October 1780 with Nathanael Greene. The Battle of Camden also took the life of Kalb, who had his horse shot out from under him, was hit eleven times by gunfire, and died on the battlefield.

✦

That summer, Washington gave Lafayette his first command in more than two years. His new unit, a handpicked light division, was put together for Lafayette and set up camp at the end of July, south of West Point on the west bank of the Hudson River. The division, which later moved into northern New Jersey, consisted of some 2,000 light infantry troops from New Hampshire, New York, Connecticut, Massachusetts, and Pennsylvania, as well as about 300 cavalrymen and a 100 riflemen—"half-savage men armed with great carbines," as Lafayette proudly described them to his brother-in-law, the Vicomte de Noailles.[14]

Lafayette couldn't have been happier with the arrangement. He spent lavishly on his men, buying them uniforms—complete with cockades, epaulets, and other accessories—and high-quality swords.

Each regiment had its own flag; for his new division, the marquis chose one made in France containing the motto *Ultimo Ratio,* loosely translated as "the Final Reckoning."

The young general led his troops through rigorous drills astride his newly purchased horse, "of a perfect whiteness and the greatest beauty," as he put it.[15] He deployed a network of spies to see what the British were up to in New Jersey and New York. His officers included General Enoch Poor, a former shipbuilder from New Hampshire; the Irish-born General Edward Hand; Lafayette's former aide Lieutenant-Colonel Jean-Joseph Sourbader de Gimat; and cavalry Lieutenant Colonel Henry ("Light Horse Harry") Lee III of Virginia, who led a 300-man light horse corps.

"The Marquis viewed this corps as one formed and modelled according to his own wishes, and as meriting his highest confidence," Continental Army physician James Thacher wrote. "They were the pride of his heart, and he was the idol of their regard, who were constantly panting for an opportunity of accomplishing some signal achievement, worthy of his and their character."[16]

However, any battlefield achievement for Lafayette's command would have to wait. He kept busy drilling his men that summer and into the fall of 1780. He also worked closely with Washington, serving as his translator and secretary in meetings with Rochambeau and Ternay—and with the Chevalier Destouches, who took over the fleet after Ternay died of a fever on December 15. Lafayette also kept up his indefatigable lobbying efforts to convince the Continental Congress and Washington to go on the offensive—and to have the French send more men and supplies.

The war, in general, went poorly that fall and winter. On September 23, the Americans learned that Benedict Arnold planned to commit what would become the most notoriously traitorous act in American military history: surrendering West Point and going over to the British Army in exchange for some 6,000 pounds. Before the American Army could arrest him, Arnold escaped down the Hudson

River on a British ship, became a brigadier general for the Crown, and eventually fought in the war against his own countrymen.

On the positive side, American militiamen and other citizen-soldiers scored a series of hit-and-run victories over Cornwallis's men in South Carolina. The most significant came on October 7, when about 1,000 militiamen, hunters, and Indian fighters under Colonels Isaac Shelby, John Sevier, William Campbell, and Charles McDowell routed British Major Patrick Ferguson, commanding some 1,200 Loyalists, on October 7 at King's Mountain, South Carolina. Another success came on January 17, 1781, when General Daniel Morgan defeated the hated British General Banastre Tarleton—who allegedly had slaughtered surrendering American troops at the Battle of Waxhaws in Cowpens, South Carolina, in May 1780.

⬧

Lafayette did manage to find some action for his light division beginning late that summer. He led his troops throughout northern New Jersey on reconnaissance and foraging missions starting in late August. In October, Lafayette planned a nighttime boat raid against British and Hessian troops on Staten Island—a "charming plan that my heart was ecstatic about for two days," he said.[17] The raid, which Washington approved, was scrapped at the last minute when a quartermaster failed to deliver the boats in time to launch the operation under cover of darkness. Not surprisingly, Lafayette was bitterly disappointed.

He kept pressing for offensive action all during the fall. In a long letter to Washington in late October, for example, Lafayette pleaded with his commander in chief to strike the British in New York, saying that doing nothing would not sit well in Versailles politically and only embolden the British. Washington, as he had been doing for months, gently chastised his aggressive young major general. "It is impossible, my dear Marquis, to desire more ardently than I do to terminate the campaign by some happy stroke," Washington wrote. "But we must consult our means rather than our wishes, and not endeavour to better our affairs by attempting things, which for want of success may make them worse."[18]

Then, on November 26, came another huge disappointment for Lafayette: Washington told him that he would be disbanding the light division and sending the men back to their state regiments. The emotional yet loyal Frenchman seemed to take the news without any undue petulance.

Washington gave his young protégé another mission: to go to Philadelphia and keep up his pressure on Congress for more supplies for the army and to support Greene in South Carolina. While Lafayette was in Philadelphia, word came just after New Year's Day 1781 of a mutiny among 2,500 troops of the Pennsylvania militia, known as the Pennsylvania Line. The hungry and angry militiamen killed two officers, wounded several others, and began marching to Philadelphia from northern New Jersey to demand their pay, which had not been forthcoming for over a year.

Congress sent Lafayette, along with John Laurens (the son of Henry Laurens) and Arthur St. Clair, the British-born general who commanded the Line, to try to calm things. They met the rebellious militiamen in Princeton, where Lafayette proved to be the voice of reason, urging the men to return to camp, promising them partial back pay and adequate food and clothing.

There was serious concern that the men would defect to the British. But the intervention by Lafayette—with help from Laurens, St. Clair, Anthony Wayne, Pennsylvania Governor Joseph Reed, and Washington—assuaged the troops' concerns.

On the other hand, a similar revolt three weeks later by the New Jersey Line at Pompton "was suppressed with more vigour" by Washington, as Lafayette put it.[19] Lafayette joined other Continental Army soldiers under the command of General Robert Howe, moving in on the mutineers on January 27, 1781. When the army surrounded the rebellious troops, they gave up without a fight. Two of the ringleaders were executed on the spot; the rest of the men were pardoned.

❧

Early February 1781 brought some good news. First, word reached Washington of Morgan's January 17 victory over Tarleton in Camden, South Carolina. Then, reports began to surface that a severe winter storm had caused significant damage to the fleet of British warships at Gardiners Bay on the eastern end of Long Island. Weather temporarily broke the English blockade, and the French, for the first time in the war, had naval superiority.

The French decided to take advantage. Destouches sent the *Eveillé*, a sixty-four-gun ship under Captain le Gardeur de Tilly, along with two other ships down the coast to face down English commerce raiders in the Chesapeake Bay. If the French could disrupt the English blockade, American merchant ships would be able to sail their cargoes of produce to Europe and help bring in much-needed cash for the struggling U.S. economy.

Washington and Lafayette saw this also as a military opportunity. The reviled Benedict Arnold, now in the employ of the British, had taken 1,600 troops and in January made a series of destructive raids on American military supply depots along the James River in Virginia—reaching as far west as Richmond. Arnold now sat in Portsmouth, Virginia, with an English fleet. Washington met with Rochambeau and Destouches in Newport, and the French agreed to send the entire fleet to the Chesapeake, along with a significant number of French troops.

Lafayette would be an important part of this plan, which by the fall would lead to the decisive battle of the Revolutionary War—one in which the Marquis de Lafayette would play a starring role.

CHAPTER 8

Great Want of Money, Baggage, and Clothing

We are next to nothing in point of opposition to so large a force.

—Marquis de Lafayette to George Washington,
May 24, 1781[1]

ON FEBRUARY 20, 1781, GEORGE WASHINGTON GAVE THE OFFICIAL ORDER
to the Marquis de Lafayette to reassemble his light infantry division,
join up with the French fleet, and try to capture Benedict Arnold in
Virginia. "When you arrive at your destination," Washington's order
said, "you must act as your own judgment and the circumstances shall
direct." If Arnold "should fall into your hands, you will execute [him]
in the most summary way."[2]

Lafayette set out with 1,200 men the next day. The group included a battalion of eight veteran companies of the First Massachusetts Regiment under Colonel Joseph Vose and Major Caleb Gibbs; a battalion under Lafayette's trusted aide Jean-Joseph Sourbader de Gimat, now a lieutenant colonel; and a battalion led by Lieutenant Colonel Francis Barber of New Jersey.

Washington sent a group of troops north in a feint, making it appear he was readying an attack on Staten Island. Meanwhile, Lafayette and his men headed south through Trenton and Philadelphia to Head of Elk, Maryland, the same spot where the British had launched their attack on Washington's troops that ended at the Battle of Brandywine in 1777.

Lafayette and his men arrived at Head of Elk on March 3. Three days later, using a flotilla of small boats put together by Commodore James Nicholson of the Continental Navy, the marquis ferried his men down the Chesapeake Bay about seventy-five miles to Annapolis, the Maryland capital.

He left the men there awaiting transport from a French frigate and, accompanied by thirty of his officers and men, headed farther down the Chesapeake in a small, armed barge. The contingent arrived on March 14 at the village of Yorktown, Virginia, perched on a bluff overlooking the south side of the York River, not far from the mouth of the Chesapeake Bay.

General Friedrich Wilhelm von Steuben, who commanded Washington's troops in Virginia, was in nearby Williamsburg. He and Lafayette immediately met and began to devise a plan to oust the British from Virginia and to capture Arnold. This was Lafayette's first time in the Tidewater region of Virginia, so he decided to get a firsthand look at the area, setting off for Williamsburg on March 16.

It was during this time that Lafayette struck up what became a warm, close friendship (at first by letter) with the state's governor, Thomas Jefferson. Aside from Lafayette's words of respect for Jefferson in his letters and thanks for what he had done to help the war effort, the marquis continued to lobby Jefferson for troop supplies. In a March 17 letter to the Sage of Monticello, for example, Lafayette said that he had been forced to impress 200 oxen from citizens to use in place of draft horses, because no one would provide the much-needed horses for his artillery.[3]

The governor commiserated with Lafayette over Virginia's less-than-stellar support for the revolutionary cause. "Mild laws, a people not used to prompt obedience, a want of provisions of war and means of procuring them render our orders often ineffectual," Jefferson said.[4]

❖

Lafayette kept up his reconnaissance of the area, crossing the James River to Suffolk, Virginia, just south of Portsmouth. There he met with von Steuben's second in command, Brigadier General John Peter Gabriel Muhlenberg, at his camp near Sleepy Hole. Both had fought together at Brandywine and Monmouth Court House.

The young French general promptly borrowed a handful of Muhlenberg's militiamen and set out to explore the area. The party soon ran into a small group of Hessian soldiers and exchanged fire. In the fight, one American was killed, two were wounded, and four were taken prisoner. This brief skirmish in late March 1781 marked the first time in almost three years that Lafayette had been under fire.

Lafayette returned to Williamsburg, still complaining about the chronic lack of supplies but buoyed by news that the entire French fleet had set sail for the Chesapeake. A group of four French warships had sailed to the Chesapeake in February, chased British Admiral Marriot Arbuthnot's ships inland, and then sailed back to Newport after capturing the British forty-four-gun heavy frigate *Romulus*.

The larger French fleet under the Chevalier Destouches left Newport on March 8, reaching the entrance to the Chesapeake Bay, just offshore from present-day Virginia Beach, on March 16. The fleet arrived only to find that a similarly sized English naval squadron under Arbuthnot had beaten them to the spot and blocked the bay. The two squadrons faced off later that day—the same day Lafayette had first arrived in Williamsburg—in the fierce Battle of Cape Henry.

When the cannonading ended, both squadrons suffered severe damage. The setback convinced Destouches to abandon his plans to attack Benedict Arnold at Portsmouth, and the French admiral sailed back to Newport. British General Henry Clinton wasted no time and sent some 2,000 troops under Major General William Phillips to join Arnold. This was the same William Phillips—Lafayette family lore had it—who had fired the shot that killed the marquis' father at the Battle of Minden in 1759.

Phillips helped Arnold resume his raiding along the James, burning tobacco warehouses; hitting American military storage facilities; and making off with wagons, clothing, livestock, horses, and other provisions. Von Steuben, Muhlenberg, and Lafayette had too few supplies and men to do anything about it.

✦

Lafayette did not find out about the Virginia Capes battle until March 25. When he did, he quickly realized that his mission in Virginia was doomed—at least for the time being. "The return of the British fleet," Lafayette wrote to Washington on March 26, "destroys every prospect of an operation against Arnold." Lafayette went on to say that he was not as concerned about the number of British troops on the ground as much as he was the presence of the British fleet. "I entertain very little hopes of seeing the French flag in Hampton Road," he wrote.[5]

Lafayette stayed in Williamsburg until March 28, and then he returned to Maryland on horseback. The marquis went out of his way to visit Washington's seventy-three-year-old mother, Mary Ball Washington, at Ferry Farm, Washington's boyhood home outside Fredericksburg, Virginia.

Lafayette reunited with his division on April 3 at Annapolis. Soon after, they began the move north to join Washington's main body of troops in New York. The marquis and his men reached Head of Elk on April 8. There he received a dispatch sent by Washington on April 6 from his headquarters near New Windsor, New York. The letter detailed Lafayette's projected role in Washington's new plan to confront the British in the South, rather than in New York. Washington ordered Lafayette to march his troops "as speedily as possible" to South Carolina "to reinforce" his friend and colleague Nathanael Greene.[6]

Many of Lafayette's still chronically undersupplied men were not exactly overjoyed when they heard the news. Some promptly deserted. Lafayette himself had mixed feelings about the plan, which he expressed in a letter to Washington.

"I am going to make every preparation to march to Virginia, so as to be ready as soon as possible," Lafayette wrote to his commander in chief. He went on to say, though, that he still "most certainly prefer[red] to be in a situation to attack New York" but didn't want his desires in that regard "to influence our determination, if this be the best way to help General Greene."[7]

On the one hand, Lafayette very much wanted to get back into action (even if it was in the South and not New York). On the other, he had just returned from Virginia and had little desire to turn his army around and head back south. Plus, he strongly believed that attacking New York should be Washington's top priority and, moreover, he suspected that Washington was planning a New York attack without him. Then there was the still-critical supply situation and the mutinous condition of his men.

Lafayette wrote to Washington on April 10, asking him to put off his move south because of "the great want of money, baggage, cloathing [*sic*], under which both officers and men are suffering."[8] Washington knew well the situation. He had sent John Laurens to France in February as a special envoy to work with Benjamin Franklin and John Adams to convince the French to do more to underwrite the Revolution with more money, supplies, and ships. Laurens had not had much luck, leading Washington to tell him in an April 9 letter that "we are at the end of our tether, and that now or never our deliverance must come."[9]

At about that same time, Lafayette wrote to the French ambassador, the Chevalier de La Luzerne, deploring the supply situation. His men, Lafayette said, had "neither money, nor clothes, nor shoes, nor shirts, and in a few days we will be reduced to eating green peaches; our feet are torn for want of shoes and our hands are covered with scabs for want of linens."[10]

La Luzerne sympathized with the young French general and wrote to Foreign Minister Comte de Vergennes on his behalf. The ambassador's lobbying, combined with John Laurens's work with Franklin and Adams in Versailles, paid dividends. Word soon came from Vergennes promising French government credit and clothing for the Continental Army but not more arms, ships, or troops. Vergennes did promise, though, that he would send part of Rear Admiral Joseph Paul François de Grasse's fleet, then in the West Indies, up to Virginia to support the land action.

This eased Lafayette's mind. So did the news that Washington was not going to attack New York but was mounting a feint in that direction to hide the fact that a large American offensive would take place in the South. Even better, from Lafayette's point of view, was the fact that he would play an integral part in the multipronged plan.

❖

Lafayette, his fears greatly allayed, on April 10 issued the order for his division to move south. His men did not react well to the news.

Several deserted. One was caught and hanged on the spot. Lafayette then issued a general order trying to reason with his men, promising them more supplies and appealing to their loyalty to him and the cause. "From that hour all desertions ceased," Lafayette wrote.[11]

The division reached the banks of the Susquehanna River in Maryland on April 12 and arrived in Baltimore a week later. Lafayette used his reputation and influence there to get credit from local merchants to the tune of 2,000 French livres (about 20,000 USD) to buy shoes, hats, and clothing for his men. That extremely generous act went a long way toward securing the loyalty of the men who would go on to fight for Lafayette in the next six months in Virginia.

The young French major general needed that allegiance because he proceeded to lead his men on a 200-mile forced march from Baltimore to Richmond. The reason for the rush: Virginia's capital city was the home to cannon and munitions factories, and Lafayette believed—with good reason—that the British planned to attack the city and seize the military hardware. Benedict Arnold, in fact, had hit Richmond in January and burned a large part of the city to the ground. He was now lurking along the James River east of the Virginia capital.

Lafayette and his men crossed the Potomac into Virginia on April 21. He wrote to Thomas Jefferson that day from Alexandria, asking for the governor's help with supplies. Lafayette called on Jefferson to arrange for "the getting of provisions" for his troops once they reached Richmond—to wit, "[b]aked bread, fresh and salt meat, with a quantity of rum." And he put in a plea for footwear. "We are so entirely destitute of shoes that [unless] a large number of them is collected, the feet of our men will be so sore as to make it impossible for them to advance."[12]

Lafayette's men reached Fredericksburg, Virginia, about halfway between Washington D.C., and Richmond, on April 25. In the interim, British Major General William Phillips's forces joined with Arnold's men, and they headed west along the James River toward

Richmond and Petersburg, twenty-five miles south of Virginia's capital. The day Lafayette's division arrived in Fredericksburg, April 25, a large contingent of British troops under Phillips defeated Generals von Steuben and Muhlenberg, commanding about 1,000 Virginia militiamen in the Battle of Petersburg, which took place near Blandford just outside the city. The Americans held out for about three hours against the 2,500-man British Army before retreating north.

The British then occupied Petersburg. Three days later, Arnold and Phillips's men marched north and routed a small group of militiamen near Manchester, Virginia, just south of Richmond. The Redcoats then set fire to buildings and ships on the James River and slaughtered livestock. Eventually, the British torched the nearby town of Chesterfield Courthouse.

The next day, April 29, Lafayette and his men reached Richmond, which was defended by only a small group of militiamen under Virginia militia commander Thomas Nelson. Arnold and Phillips approached the city the following day. They were about to cross the James when they saw Lafayette and his division arrayed on a hill overlooking the river. The British thought better of attacking and headed back down the James to Petersburg. Their plan was to wait and fight another day with the addition of significant numbers of troops from Cornwallis's army, which was en route to Virginia from North Carolina.

Lafayette and von Steuben considered that face-off in Richmond a victory. They celebrated by putting on a grand review of Continental Army troops for the city's citizens. Lafayette also continued to lobby Virginia Governor Thomas Jefferson—whom he had now met face to face for the first time in Richmond—for supplies and men. Although those were not forthcoming, the two men conversed in French and Latin, discussed worldly and philosophical matters, and greatly enjoyed each other's company.

After the merriment in Richmond ended, Lafayette took his men to Bottoms Bridge, about ten miles east of the city, on the road to Williamsburg and Jamestown. It was there that he received the official word from Nathanael Greene that he would not be going to South Carolina but would instead be put in charge of all Continental troops in Virginia.

"I have only one word of advice to give you (having entire confidence in your ability, zeal and good conduct)," Greene said in that dispatch, "that is not to let the love of fame get the better of your prudence and plunge you into misfortune, in too eager a pursuit after glory."[13]

Phillips, meanwhile, had moved his men to Jamestown—the island site of the first permanent English settlement in North America off the north bank of the James River, about forty miles from the mouth of the Chesapeake. He didn't stay there long. Phillips shortly thereafter received orders to go back to Petersburg to meet Cornwallis and his troops.

When he arrived in Petersburg on May 10, Phillips fell seriously ill, suffering most likely from typhus. Lafayette, meanwhile, had moved his artillery outside of Petersburg and that day opened fire on the town. Three days later, Phillips died of fever, and Arnold took command of all British forces in Virginia. Arnold tried to communicate with Lafayette, sending him a note suggesting a prisoner exchange. Lafayette pointedly ignored it. He very much wanted to hang Arnold, not bargain with him.

But Lafayette had to stifle his aggressive impulses because he simply did not have enough troops (less than 1,000 at that point) to face the British in a set battle. Plus, he felt extreme loyalty to his commanding officer, Nathanael Greene, who had ordered him to avoid a face-to-face confrontation with the British.

"Though young and enterprising, La Fayette was too sagacious to have risked the bold measure of occupying Petersburg, even had he been free to act as his own judgment might direct," Henry Lee later wrote, "but acting as he did in a subordinate character [to Greene], he never could have been induced to violate orders."[14]

In Lafayette's "difficult situation," Lee noted, "it was necessary to preserve appearances, to keep the country in good spirits, as well as to render his soldiers strict in attention to duty, never so susceptible of discipline as when impressed with the conviction that battle is at hand."[15]

Lafayette returned to the Richmond area, setting up camp north of the James where he waited for reinforcements in the form of 800 troops from Pennsylvania who were heading south under Brigadier General Anthony Wayne. British intelligence falsely reported that Wayne had joined Lafayette, and Arnold therefore decided not to move against the Americans until all of Cornwallis's men had arrived from North Carolina.

Cornwallis finally arrived on May 20 with some 1,500 men and joined Arnold at Petersburg. The British lieutenant general now had some 7,200 troops under his command. One of his goals was to take Lafayette prisoner and send him back in humiliation to England. "I shall now proceed to dislodge Lafayette from Richmond," Cornwallis wrote to Henry Clinton in New York. "The boy," he said, "cannot escape me."[16]

It looked as though Cornwallis's prediction would come true. Lafayette faced overwhelmingly difficult odds. He had at his command just over 900 Continental Army troops, augmented by fewer than 2,000 militiamen under Muhlenberg and Nelson, and just six artillery pieces.

"I am wavering between two inconveniences," Lafayette wrote to Washington in late May. "Were I to fight a battle, I should be cut to pieces, the militia dispersed, and the arms lost. Were I to decline fighting, the country would think itself given up." Lafayette felt his only recourse was to shadow the British and make hit-and-run attacks on them. "I am therefore determined to skirmish," he told Washington, "but not to engage too far, and particularly to take care against their immense and excellent body of horse, whom the militia fear as they would so many wild beasts."[17]

The supply situation remained dire. "The various [states] give me more trouble than Lord Cornwallis," Lafayette said in a letter to the

Comte de Noailles. "We haven't a crown, we are spending immense sums, and we are short of everything."[18]

Lafayette left Richmond, as did the Virginia General Assembly, which took off to Charlottesville, seventy miles to the west, in the last two weeks of May. From late May until early August, Lafayette delivered on his promise to skirmish with, but not engage, the British. He constantly moved his men efficiently and effectively through the heavily wooded areas north, west, and east of Richmond and along the Virginia Peninsula on rough roads and even rougher trails. His men continued to harass, elude, and frustrate Cornwallis's much-larger forces.

In late May, Benedict Arnold received orders to leave Virginia and head back north. Cornwallis chased Lafayette's men north of Richmond in early June and then withdrew after Wayne's 800 Pennsylvanians finally joined Lafayette on June 10. The marquis gave chase, putting his men through a forced march toward the James River.

"On our gaining the South Anna [River] we found Lord Cornwallis encamped some miles below the point of fork," Lafayette later reported to Greene. "A stolen march through a difficult road gave us a position…between the enemy and our magazines, where, agreeable to appointment, we were joined by a body of riflemen. The next day Lord Cornwallis retired towards Richmond (where he now is) and was followed by our small army."[19]

For several weeks, intermittent skirmishes took place between American militiamen and some of Cornwallis's troops under General Banastre Tarleton and Lieutenant Colonel John G. Simcoe. In late June, Cornwallis received an order from Clinton to send about half of his troops to New York. On July 4, 1781, while Lafayette and his men celebrated American Independence Day, Cornwallis left Williamsburg en route to Jamestown, where he would cross the James and send the northbound troops to their embarkation point at Portsmouth.

Lafayette, going on false information provided by British spies, decided to attack Cornwallis's rear guard and ordered Wayne and his men to do so. The July 6 Battle of Green Spring, northwest of Jamestown, turned out to be the last significant fight on the Virginia Peninsula until the showdown at Yorktown in September and October. This prelude to Yorktown did not go well for the Americans, although some daring fighting by Wayne and his troops avoided what could have been a catastrophic defeat.

Cornwallis only sent a few troops across the James, keeping the bulk of his army behind and hoping that Lafayette would fall for the deception. He did. The marquis, who accompanied Wayne on the mission, only realized at the last moment that he would be facing many more troops than he was led to believe. Before he could withdraw, the British attacked.

Anthony Wayne's 800 men and three cannons went head to head with more than 2,000 enemy troops. Wayne ordered a daring—some say foolishly impetuous—bayonet charge and then, with Lafayette's help under fire, managed an orderly retreat. The British suffered some 75 casualties and the Americans about 140.

Twenty-year-old Ebenezer Denny, then a lieutenant in the Fourth Pennsylvania Regiment, offered a vivid description of the battle in his military journal. After his captain was wounded, Denny wrote, "the charge of the company devolved on me; young and inexperienced, exhausted with hunger and fatigue." Denny feared he would "like to have disgraced" himself, he said, because he "had [eaten] nothing all day but a few blackberries [and] was faint, and with difficulty kept my place." Several times, "[I] was about to throw away my arms (a very heavy espontoon [spear])."[20]

But Denny persevered, leading his company, which consisted of "almost all old soldiers." They "kept compact and close to our leading company, and continued running until out of reach of the fire. The enemy advanced no farther than to the ground we left." The fight, he wrote, lasted only about three or four minutes. Denny noted that aside from the American troops killed, wounded, and captured, the regiment also lost two artillery horses and two cannons.[21]

The numbers signified a clear British victory. But the Americans took heart at the courage under fire displayed by their fellow soldiers and officers. In a letter to Noailles a few days later, Lafayette was reflective and humble. "The devil Cornwallis is much wiser than the other generals with whom I have dealt," he wrote. "He inspires me with a sincere fear, and his name has greatly troubled my sleep." The Virginia campaign, he said, "is a good school for me. God grant that the public does not pay for my lessons."[22]

After the brief, fierce fight at Green Spring, Cornwallis finished his move across the James. Within ten days, he had his troops ready to ship out to New York from Portsmouth. Then on July 21, Cornwallis received an order from Clinton telling him to keep all of his troops in Virginia and do everything he could to hold the strategically important peninsula sitting between the York and James Rivers. Cornwallis decided to make the small village of Yorktown his base of operations.

The British high command approved. His most senior officers advised General Henry Clinton, the commander in chief in America, that Yorktown was readily defensible and easily reinforced by sea. Yorktown could "be defended with the troops [Cornwallis] then had against twenty thousand assailants for at least three weeks after opened trenches," Clinton later wrote. This was mainly because Yorktown and its defenses occupied "a space of ground somewhat higher than that round it, between two impracticable ravines ascending from the river."[23]

At the end of July, the British shipped some 4,500 men from Portsmouth to Yorktown, where they arrived on August 1. Throughout the month of August, more British forces arrived, including Tarleton and his men and horses. The British began building defenses at Yorktown and at Gloucester across the York River.

In 1781, Lafayette spent the month of August trying to discern what the British were up to. After Green Spring, he had Wayne follow Cornwallis. At one point, Lafayette believed that Cornwallis was heading to Baltimore from Portsmouth and began moving his division north. But with the help of James Armistead, a Virginia slave who volunteered to serve as a Continental Army spy, Lafayette learned the truth. Posing as an escaped slave, Armistead had infiltrated Cornwallis's camp at Yorktown. The marquis then moved most of his division to a camp on the Pamunkey River near West Point, Virginia, east of Williamsburg. He kept Wayne's Pennsylvania Line south of the James.

❖

With those forces in place and with Cornwallis hunkered down at Yorktown, Washington came up with a bold plan. Lafayette would block the British from the west, General von Steuben would move in from the southwest and Greene from the south. The French fleet would bottle up the English at the mouth of the Chesapeake. Washington would move most of his and Comte de Rochambeau's forces—about 8,800 men—down from New York and completely surround the British.

An important element of Washington's strategy was keeping Cornwallis in Yorktown. It "will be of great importance towards the success of our present enterprise that the enemy on the arrival of the fleet, should not have it in their power to effect their retreat," Washington wrote to Lafayette on August 18. "I cannot omit to repeat to you my most earnest wish, that the land and Naval Force which you will have with you may so combine their operations, that the British Army may not be able to escape you." Washington ended the letter with fulsome praise for Lafayette's military acumen, saying, "I am persuaded your military genius and judgment will lead you to make the best improvement."[24]

In December 1776, the nineteen-year-old Marquis de Lafayette met in Paris with the German-born French Army officer Johan de Kalb (center) and Silas Deane (right). (Alonzo Chappel, artist [New York, circa 1856]. From the collections of the Society of the Cincinnati, Washington, D.C.)

The Battle of Brandywine, September 11, 1777. A British musket ball tore into Lafayette's left calf. After being helped back onto his horse, he led the men on an orderly retreat. (Engraved by Charles Henry Jeens after Alonso Chappel [New York, 1861]. From the Robert Charles Lawrence Fergusson Collection, the Society of the Cincinnati, Washington, D.C.)

Lafayette spent the infamously cold winter of 1777–78 with George Washington at Valley Forge. (Engraved by Henry Bryan Hall after Alonso Chappel [New York, circa 1856]. From the collections of the Society of the Cincinnati, Washington, D.C.)

Lafayette (next to George Washington, pointing) played an important role on Washington's staff during the Siege at Yorktown, and in the months leading up that famed battle. (Marquis de Lafayette Collection, Skillman Library, Lafayette College)

Lafayette depicted with James Armistead, a slave in Virginia who volunteered to serve as a Continental Army spy and, posing as an escaped slave, infiltrated Cornwallis's camp at Yorktown. (Marquis de Lafayette Collection, Skillman Library, Lafayette College)

Eighteenth-century map of the Battle of Yorktown. (Published by Isaac Collins [Trenton, 1785]. From the Robert Charles Lawrence Fergusson Collection, the Society of the Cincinnati, Washington, D.C.)

Gilbert Motier Marquis de
LA FAYETTE

Lafayette in France following the American Revolution. (Marquis de Lafayette Collection, Skillman Library, Lafayette College)

King Louis XVI, the ineffectual French monarch whom Lafayette had known since his marriage into the aristocratic Noailles family in 1773. (Engraved by Jean-Guillaume Bervic after Antoine-Francois Callet [later impression from original Paris, 1790 plate]. From the collections of the Society of the Cincinnati, Washington, D.C.

Lafayette during the French Revolution.
(Marquis de Lafayette Collection,
Skillman Library, Lafayette College)

Adrienne Lafayette and her two daughters Anastasie and Virginie. (Reproduced by permission of The Society of the Cincinnati, Washington, D.C.)

Lafayette returned to a rapturous welcome during his 1824–25 visit to all 24 American states. (Marquis de Lafayette Collection, Skillman Library, Lafayette College)

The Marquis was front and center during the July Revolution of 1830, during which the French overthrew the autocratic Charles X in favor of Louis-Philippe. (Marquis de Lafayette Collection, Skillman Library, Lafayette College)

Lafayette embraced Louis-Philippe—until late in 1830 when the king and Chamber of Deputies became too authoritarian in his eyes. (Marquis de Lafayette Collection, Skillman Library, Lafayette College)

Lafayette in his seventies. The marquis died on May 20, 1834, four months short of his seventy-seventh birthday. (Marquis de Lafayette Collection, Skillman Library, Lafayette College)

CHAPTER 9

Yorktown: The Fifth Act

Heavy fire from our batteries all day. A shell from one of the French mortars set fire to a British frigate; she burnt to the water's edge, and blew up, made the earth shake. Shot and shell raked the town in every direction.

—Continental Army Lieutenant Ebenezer Denny, October 15, 1781[1]

GEORGE WASHINGTON AND COMTE DE ROCHAMBEAU LEARNED IN mid-August 1781 that Rear Admiral Joseph Paul François de Grasse had begun to move his formidable fleet out of the West Indies on the way to the Chesapeake Bay. Grasse's fleet included twenty-eight ships of the line armed with some 1,700 cannons, three frigates, a good number of transport vessels, and some 3,250 troops commanded by the Marquis de Saint-Simon. Washington and Rochambeau quickly gave the order to their armies in New York to strike their camps and head south.

The order, issued on August 15, was vague; Washington deliberately kept the troops in the dark about their final destination to keep the British guessing. Rumors along the march had it that the Continental Army would be attacking the British in New York City and on Long Island, which is what Washington wanted the enemy to think. It was not until August 22 when the army had marched past Princeton, New Jersey, that it became obvious what the objective was: a 500-mile trek to Virginia.

"Our destination can no longer be a secret," army surgeon Dr. James Thacher wrote in his diary that day. "The British army under Lord Cornwallis is unquestionably the object of our present expedition. It is now rumored that a French fleet may soon be expected to arrive in Chesapeake Bay, to cooperate with the allied army in that quarter."[2]

In Virginia, the Marquis de Lafayette had been ordered to keep General Charles Cornwallis bottled up in the small river village of Yorktown—and to feed, clothe, and arm his American and French troops. He succeeded at both tasks but not without many anxious moments, especially with regard to the perpetually unreliable supply situation.

"We are destitute of ammunition, and the army living from hand to mouth," Lafayette wrote on August 30 to Governor Thomas Nelson, who had succeeded Thomas Jefferson as Virginia's chief executive. It was an "unhappy situation," Lafayette told Nelson—a situation that easily could result in Cornwallis escaping into North Carolina. That state of affairs, Lafayette said, would "end in the disgrace and destruction of the American troops in this State; and have the most decisive effects against American independence."[3]

The day before Lafayette wrote that letter, on August 29, 1781, Admiral de Grasse's French fleet had arrived at the mouth of the

Chesapeake Bay. Not long after, the fifty-nine-year-old Grasse began pushing for an immediate attack on Cornwallis. Lafayette uncharacteristically advocated caution. He was nearby in Williamsburg and told Grasse that Washington and Rochambeau's men would soon be arriving in Virginia, and "it was far better to hasten their movements than act without them." Lafayette wrote in his memoirs that if he had listened to Grasse, "a murderous attack" would have resulted which might have "shed a great deal of blood from a feeling of vanity and a selfish love of glory.[4]

It was apparent that the twenty-three-year-old Frenchman had made marked strides as a leader during his four years in America. He had tamed his youthful aggressive tendencies. The marquis was able to formulate strategy and tactics as situations warranted—as in this case when he wisely urged caution.

Lafayette told Grasse that he was certain that after the American and French troops arrived in Virginia, they would be able to take Cornwallis "by a regular attack, and thus spare the lives of the soldiers, which a good general ought always to respect as much as possible, especially in a country where it was so difficult to obtain others to replace those who fell."[5]

While Lafayette argued to leave nothing to chance, a naval battle took place at the mouth of the Chesapeake Bay that would have important consequences in the American and French effort against Cornwallis at Yorktown. Known as the Second Battle of the Virginia Capes, or the Battle of the Chesapeake, the bulk of the fighting took place on September 5, 1781, in the waters between Capes Henry and Charles. Grasse and his fleet of twenty-four French ships of the line armed with some 1,700 cannons and 19,000 seamen squared off against British Admiral Thomas Graves and his nineteen ships with roughly 1,400 cannons and 13,000 sailors.

The two sides maneuvered and exchanged vicious broadside fire on September 5 and intermittently for the next two days. Both fleets suffered extensive damage; the British had 90 killed and 246 wounded; the French took about 200 total casualties. Grasse prevailed; Graves went back to New York for repairs, and the French navy now had a vital element of the broader plan in place: sealing Cornwallis in by sea.

On September 10, a small squadron of French naval ships under the Comte de Barras headed up the York River. Barras brought with him much-needed siege cannons and other arms and ammunition for the French and Americans to use in their assault on Cornwallis at Yorktown.

Two days after the sea battle, on September 7, the day after his twenty-fourth birthday, Lafayette moved his men to Williamsburg, west of Yorktown. The next day, Lafayette's division gained 3,250 additional fighting men when the Marquis de Saint-Simon, the commander of the French troops that Grasse had on his fleet, joined them.

The French troops "make a very fine, soldierly appearance, they being all very tall men," First Lieutenant William Feltman of the First Pennsylvania Regiment wrote in his journal. "Their uniform is white coats turned up with blue, their underclothes are white."[6]

❖

From Williamsburg, Lafayette detached reconnaissance parties and maintained his network of spies. The marquis soon received a clearer picture of what Cornwallis had been up to since the British general had moved his men into the village of Yorktown on August 1.

A large number of former slaves, who had joined the British in the hope of winning freedom, did most of the labor building up Yorktown's defenses. Cornwallis was "working day and night and will soon work himself into a respectable situation," Lafayette wrote to Washington on September 8. "He has taken on shore the greatest part of his sailors. He is picking up whatever provisions he can get.... Our present position will render him cautious."[7]

Meanwhile, Washington; Rochambeau, his second in command; the Chevalier de Chastellux; and their aides had left their army at

Head of Elk, Maryland, where the men would wait for French ships to take them down the Chesapeake. The commanding officers raced south on horseback, reaching Mount Vernon on September 10.

They then rode to Williamsburg, a distance of about 150 miles, arriving four days later. Not long after he arrived in the former Virginia capital, General Washington and his all-but-adopted French son had an emotional reunion. "Never was more joy painted in any countenances than theirs," Colonel St. George Tucker, Governor Nelson's liaison with the French Army, wrote to his wife the next day. "The Marquis rode up with precipitation, clasped the General in his arms and embraced him with an ardor not easily described."[8]

Lafayette was not the only one thrilled with Washington's arrival. The troops fired off a twenty-one-cannon salute that afternoon in Washington's honor, and as Lieutenant William Feltman put it, "there was a universal joy amongst our officers and soldiers, especially the French troops, on his arrival."[9]

Washington now took command of the American and French forces on the Virginia Peninsula. "Officers all pay their respects to the Commander-in-chief," Ebenezer Denny wrote in his war journal on September 15. "He stands in the door, takes every man by the hand—the officers all pass in, receiving his salute and shake.... The presence of so many general officers, and the arrival of new corps, seem to give additional life to everything; discipline the order of the day."[10]

❖

On September 17, 1781, Washington, Rochambeau, Chastellux, Henry Knox, and Washington's chief engineer, the Chevalier Duportail, boarded the tender *Queen Charlotte* and sailed in a rainstorm to Cape Henry. There they held a council of war with Grasse aboard the French fleet's massive, three-decked, 110-gun flagship, the *Ville de Paris*.

It was not an entirely happy occasion. Grasse, believing a British fleet was on the way from New York, told Washington that he was about to leave and sail back to the French West Indies. Washington was not pleased. "Your Excellency's departure from the Chesapeake, by affording an opening for the succour of York, which the enemy would instantly avail themselves of, would frustrate these brilliant prospects," he wrote to Grasse a week later. The consequences of that, Washington said, "would be not only the disgrace and loss of renouncing an enterprise... after the most expensive preparations and uncommon exertions and fatigues, but perhaps the disbanding of the whole army for want of provisions."[11]

Washington dispatched Lafayette to deliver the dire warning and to try to convince Grasse to stay. Lafayette boarded Grasse's flagship on September 26. Again, Washington entrusted him with a vital mission. The powerful French fleet blocking the Chesapeake Bay was a critical part of the planned assault on Yorktown. Without it, Washington had little hope of defeating Cornwallis.

"The whole expedition seemed on the point of failing," Lafayette wrote later, "and General Washington begged Lafayette to go on board the admiral's ship in the bay, and endeavour to persuade him to change his mind." Lafayette did not let Washington down. He succeeded in convincing Grasse to stay put. And "the siege of Yorktown," Lafayette said, "was begun."[12]

The siege officially began a week after Washington and Rochambeau's troops finally reached the peninsula on September 20, 1781, after their land-and-sea trek from New York. In the next few days, the men unloaded the cannons and other military equipment from the French ships.

By the last week of September, the Americans and French had assembled a formidable fighting force. Altogether, Washington had about 5,700 Continental Army soldiers, some 3,200 militiamen, and roughly 7,500 French troops. Washington organized his command into three divisions, under Generals Lafayette, Friedrich Wilhelm von

Steuben, and Benjamin Lincoln. Washington's plan was to array the American units on the right and the French troops on the left.

Washington chose the forty-eight-year-old Lincoln—who had been disgraced at Charleston but was the senior general—to have overall command of the three American divisions. That did not go over well with Lafayette, who felt he deserved the honor. Command "of the Right Wing in the Siege is of the highest importance to me," Lafayette said, "as it cannot have any similar effect upon...Lincoln's reputation and military prospects in Europe and the future course of his life."[13] Lafayette's plea fell on deaf ears, and the command structure remained as Washington planned it.

The order of battle also included several artillery detachments, companies of sappers and miners, and other units under Henry Knox. Irish-born Colonel Stephen Moylan of Pennsylvania led the Continental cavalry—the Fourth Regiment of the Continental Light Dragoons, part of Lafayette's light division. Virginia Governor Nelson himself commanded the militiamen, supported by his brigade commanders (and fellow Virginians) Brigadier Generals George Weedon, Robert Lawson, and Edward Stevens.

Rochambeau led the French troops, which made up more than half of the ground forces arrayed against Cornwallis. He had seven infantry regiments grouped in three brigades. His commanders included the Duc de Lauzun, who led Lauzun's Legion of cavalrymen; Colonel Commandant d'Aboville, the chief of artillery; and Colonel Commandant Desandrouins, the head of the engineer detachments. Rochambeau's *maréchal de camp* was Brigadier General Claude-Gabriel, the Duc de Choisy.[14]

Cornwallis, hunkered down in his newly built works at Yorktown, faced the massed French and American troops with about 10,000 soldiers and sailors.

❖

At 5:00 A.M. on September 28, the Americans and French moved out from Williamsburg toward Yorktown. Washington and Rochambeau set up their headquarters south of Yorktown on the east side of Beaverdam Creek, within cannonading distance of the British outer defense line. Washington arrayed his troops in a six-mile semicircle around Yorktown, with Lafayette's light infantry division on the far right and Rochambeau's on the left. Across the mile-wide York River on Gloucester Point, British general Banastre Tarleton was bottled in by some 1,500 Virginia militiamen under General Weedon, 600 cavalrymen of Lauzun's Legion, and a contingent of 800 French marines under General Choisy, who took command of the allied force there on September 30.

After some minor picket and cannon fire on the afternoon of September 28, all guns at Yorktown went quiet. Cornwallis received a dispatch from General Henry Clinton that evening saying that a significant number of British troops would be leaving New York on October 5 to come to Cornwallis's aid.

Cornwallis reacted by ordering all of his men back into the Yorktown works and sending his commanding officer a letter, confidently saying that he would be able to fend off the Americans and French if the reinforcements arrived in a reasonable amount of time. By dawn the next morning, the British had moved all of their troops into the immediate defenses of Yorktown.

The Redcoats hunkered down inside a series of seven redoubts and earthworks linked by trenches. A high, earthen work parapet protected the rear stockade. Behind them, the British had fourteen batteries containing sixty-five guns. The redoubts, earthworks, and trenches were studded with pointed inclined stakes, called "fraising," and mounds of felled trees with sharpened branches pointed outward, known as "abatis."

Cornwallis felt safe on his right and center because of a virtually impenetrable, deep and wide marshy ravine between him and the Americans and French—and the presence of a heavily fortified star redoubt near the York River. There also was another defensive structure: a horn work (a pair of half bastions connected by a curtain wall) close in to the main fortification, along with a ditch and more fraising and abatis.

The French and Americans promptly moved into the outer fortifications the English had abandoned. A French detachment took advantage of the situation and probed the star fort, only to be repulsed by pickets of the Twenty-Third Regiment, the Welsh Fusiliers. Otherwise, things were quiet that day.

"Scarce a gun fired this day," Washington's secretary, Colonel Jonathan Trumbull of Connecticut, wrote in his journal on September 30. We "find ourselves very unexpectedly upon very advantageous ground, commanding their line of works in near approach.... At night our troops begin to throw up some works and to take advantage of the enemies' evacuated labours."[15]

"The enemy remain within their inner fortifications," Lafayette wrote to French Ambassador Chevalier de La Luzerne that same day, and "we are also drawing closer to them than we could have hoped." The operation, Lafayette said, "will soon be noisy."[16]

The next day, October 1, 1781, the Americans began building a redoubt and battery of their own. They also made a series of zig-zagging, protective trenches, called parallel lines, that would be dug closer and closer to the British lines—the basis for Washington and Rochambeau's strategy: a classic European siege.

"The engineers stroll about like sorcerers making circles around poor Cornwallis," Lafayette wrote to La Luzerne on October 3, "and the general officers train their spyglasses, awaiting the moment to take the trench."[17]

The British, meanwhile, buttressed their defenses (still believing reinforcements were on the way) by reinforcing their redoubts on their left. Cornwallis ordered Tarleton and some of his cavalry and mounted infantry to cross the York River from Gloucester to join him in Yorktown.

The noise that Lafayette mentioned first came from the British, who unleashed heavy cannon and mortar fire for two days, October

1 and 2, trying to disrupt the French and American siege work. Lauzan's Legion also skirmished with British troops near Gloucester. There were some American and French casualties in both engagements. The shelling, though, did not significantly delay the siege setting. The British also scuttled four ships in the York to try to prevent an American sea landing.

❖

On October 6, with the first parallel line in place about 600 yards from the British defenses, the siege began. The French and American guns began whipping the British positions and continued around the clock for three days. Washington himself personally fired the first shot. The Americans took very few casualties. We "will pound the defenses so as to put them in a very bad condition," Lafayette reported to La Luzerne.[18]

Ebenezer Denny wrote in his journal on October 9: "Our cannon and mortars began to play. The scene viewed from the camp now was grand, particularly after dark—a number of shells from the works of both parties passing high in the air, and descending in a curve, each with a long train of fire, exhibited a brilliant spectacle." The troops in the three American divisions took turns digging new trenches. "We were two nights in camp and one in the lines," Denny reported. [19]

On October 10, both sides let loose more heavy cannonading. Lafayette's division put four new batteries into action that day. The largest consisted of sixteen 18- and 24-pound guns and six mortars and howitzers. One French battery on the left had six 13-inch mortars, an American-manned battery had four 10-inch mortars, and another battery had four 18-pounders.[20]

Cornwallis felt the heat and wondered when the troops Clinton had promised would arrive. He sent a dispatch to Clinton on October 11, asking what had happened to the promised reinforcements. "Nothing but a direct move to York River, which includes a successful naval action, can save me," Cornwallis said.[21]

That day, the French and Americans finished building their new artillery batteries and brought forward more cannons, heavy mortars, and howitzers. "A tremendous fire now opened from all the new works, French and American," Denny wrote that day. "The heavy cannon directed against the embrasures and guns of the enemy. Their pieces were soon silenced, broke and dismantled."[22]

Continental Army surgeon James Thacher, who served with the men in the trenches, wrote about the barrage in his journal.

> I have a fine opportunity of witnessing the sublime and stupendous scene which is continually exhibiting. The bomb shells from the besiegers and the besieged are incessantly crossing each others' path in the air. They are clearly visible in the form of a black ball in the day, but in the night, they appear like fiery meteors with blazing tails, most beautifully brilliant, ascending majestically from the mortar to a certain altitude, and gradually descending to the spot where they are destined to execute their work of destruction. It is astonishing with what accuracy an experienced gunner will make his calculations, that a shell shall fall within a few feet of a given point, and burst at the precise time, though at a great distance. When a shell falls, it whirls round, burrows, and excavates the earth to a considerable extent, and bursting, makes dreadful havoc around. I have more than once witnessed fragments of the mangled bodies and limbs of the British soldiers thrown into the air by the bursting of our shells.[23]

The Americans and French soon realized that the key to winning the siege would be to take the two redoubts, numbers 9 and 10, near the York River on the Americans' right—the side manned by Lafayette's division. Redoubt number 10, on the edge of a bluff overlooking the river, was held by about seventy British troops armed with muskets, bayonets, and cannons. Redoubt number 9, a five-sided structure closer inland, was defended by some 125 Hessian and British troops.

The artillery pounded the redoubts for two days. On the night of October 14, 1781, Washington addressed 400 of Lafayette's men—something he rarely did. He told them the importance of taking the redoubts and readied them for a bayonet charge. He then ordered feints on the left and at Gloucester across the York. Then, at 8:00 P.M., the attack on redoubts 9 and 10 began.

The night, Ebenezer Denny noted, "was dark and favorable. Our batteries had ceased, there appeared to be a dead calm; we followed the infantry and halted about half way, kept a few minutes in suspense, when we were ordered to advance."[24]

Lafayette chose Colonel Jean-Joseph Sourbader de Gimat's battalion to lead the assault, supported by Lieutenant Colonel Hamilton's battalion, with Hamilton in command of the mission. Some eighty men under Lieutenant Colonel John Laurens also were in the mix, as was a detachment of sappers and miners, and a contingent of troops under Major Nicholas Fish.

The troops moved in two columns on a quarter-mile, fixed-bayonet charge. The men hit the edges of the redoubt and plowed right through the tangled abatis without stopping. Within ten minutes, the fighting ended. Nine Americans were killed and thirty-one were wounded, but the redoubt was in American hands without the attacking troops firing a shot.

Thacher provided this first-person account in his war journal:

> The assailants bravely entered the fort with the point of the bayonet without firing a single gun...Colonel Gimat received a slight wound in his foot....[British] Major Campbell, who commanded in the fort, was wounded and taken prisoner, with about thirty soldiers, the remainder made their escape. I was desired to visit the wounded in the fort, even before the balls had ceased whistling about my ears, and saw a sergeant and eight men dead in the ditch....During the assault, the British kept

up an incessant firing of cannon and musketry from their whole line.

Some 400 French grenadiers and chasseurs under the Comte Colonel Guillaume Deux-Ponts then went after redoubt number 9. In this case, the enemy met the French with a charge. The French countercharged and prevailed but only after a bloody fight in which they suffered nearly a hundred casualties.

While the fighting continued that night, American troops dug the second and last parallel line. They also shored up the lines with bundles of dried wood, called "fascines." "We were very much exposed to the enemy's fire, both musquetry and cannon balls and grape shot, and not a single man hurt," William Feltman wrote in his journal the next day.[25]

By the following morning, October 15, the Americans had finished work on the second parallel, sitting just 300 yards from Yorktown. The line included the former British redoubts. Now the French and Americans had nearly a hundred cannons, mortars, and howitzers trained on Cornwallis's men, who had their backs to the York River.

Dr. Thacher wrote in his war journal: "The whole peninsula trembles under the incessant thunderings of our infernal machines. We have leveled some of their works in ruins and silenced their guns; they have almost ceased firing. We are so near as to have a distinct view of the dreadful havoc and destruction of their works, and even see the men in their lines torn to pieces by the bursting of our shells." The "scene," Thacher said, "is drawing to a close."[26]

Cornwallis knew it, too. "My situation now becomes very critical," he wrote to Clinton. "We shall soon be exposed to an assault, in ruined works, in a bad position and with weakened numbers. The safety of the place is therefore so precarious that I cannot recommend that the fleet and army should run great risque in endeavouring to save us."[27]

But Cornwallis was not quite ready to give up. Late on the night of October 15, he ordered an attack against the second parallel line. Some 350 men under Lieutenant Colonel Robert Abercrombie moved out near the center of the line, took a few surprised Continentals prisoner, and destroyed some American guns. But a group of French grenadiers under Vicomte de Noailles soon beat back Abercrombie and his men in the early morning hours of October 16.

During the night on October 16, Cornwallis tried to escape the only way that was open, to the north. He ordered all able-bodied and wounded troops to get ready to cross the York River to Gloucester Point in sixteen large boats. The idea was that after crossing the York, the British would make a quick march north to the safe haven of New York.

It never happened. Several boats made it across the river. But then a violent storm of rain and wind suddenly blew up, driving all of Cornwallis's boats—including those with troops onboard—downstream.

"It was soon evident that the intended passage was impracticable," Cornwallis later wrote.[28] He had to abandon the escape plan—and the battle. Cornwallis suffered some 550 casualties (killed, wounded, and taken prisoner) versus about 275 for the French and 260 for the Americans. Making matters worse, many of his men were sick with fever.

❖

At 10:00 A.M. the next morning, October 17, 1781, Cornwallis waved a white flag of surrender. He sent a note to Washington proposing a twenty-four-hour cease-fire while two officers from each side negotiated the surrender terms. Washington gave him two hours to present his terms in writing. The reply came, and the negotiations took place the next day at the home of Augustine Moore, just behind the first siege line. The Vicomte de Noailles and John Laurens represented

George Washington, and the duo hammered out an agreement with their British counterparts.

At Lafayette's insistence, and with Laurens's strong support, the British agreed to the same surrender terms that they had forced upon the Americans at Charleston: the surrendering troops would march out with, as Thacher put it, "shouldered arms, colors cased and drums beating a British or German march, and...ground their arms at a place assigned for the purpose."[29] Washington agreed with those and the other terms, and the commanding generals signed the surrender documents the following day, October 19.

The formal surrender took place at 2:00 P.M. as the British marched out of Yorktown in new uniforms. Cornwallis chose not to appear, saying he was ill. Brigadier General Charles O'Hara, Cornwallis's second in command, did the honors for the British.

"The road through which they marched was lined with spectators, French and American," Henry Lee, who was present, later wrote. "On one side the commander-in-chief, surrounded by his suite and the American staff, took his station; on the other side, opposite to him, was the Count de Rochambeau in like manner attended." The British Army approached, Lee said, "moving slowly in column with grace and precision. Universal silence was observed amidst the vast concourse, and the utmost decency prevailed."[30]

The French troops, "in complete uniform, displayed a martial and noble appearance," James Thacher, also an eyewitness, wrote in his journal. "The Americans, though not all in uniform nor their dress so neat, yet exhibited an erect soldierly air, and every countenance beamed with satisfaction and joy." A large number of citizens showed up to witness the surrender, "in point of numbers probably equal to the military, but universal silence and order prevailed," Thacher reported. O'Hara "was followed by the conquered troops in a slow and solemn step, with shouldered arms, colors cased and drums beating a British march."[31]

The next day, October 20, 1781, Lafayette wrote to French Prime Minister Comte de Maurepas: "The play is over, Monsieur le Comte. The fifth act has just ended. I was a bit uneasy during the first acts, but my heart keenly enjoyed the last one."[32]

CHAPTER 10

America, Sure of Her Independence

Our old warriors admire you; the young ones want to take you as a model.

—French Minister of War Marquis de Ségur to
Lafayette, December 5, 1781[1]

ALTHOUGH IT TOOK TWO MORE YEARS AFTER THE BATTLE OF YORKTOWN to negotiate and sign a peace treaty, the Revolutionary War ended when General Charles Cornwallis's troops surrendered. Even though the British still had some 26,000 troops in the United States and controlled the important Atlantic Coast port cities of New York, Charleston, Savannah, and Wilmington, there would be no more battles between George Washington's Continental Army and the British.

British Prime Minister Frederick Lord North, a strong supporter of the war who had been in office since 1770, suffered a parliamentary vote of no confidence after Yorktown and was forced to resign in March 1782. Sir Henry Clinton, the commander in chief of British forces, was recalled and replaced. Pro-war sentiment in England waned to the point where the government suspended all military activity in America.

Two days after the Yorktown surrender ceremony, British and Hessian troops were taken to prisoner-of-war camps in Virginia and Maryland. As for Cornwallis and the general officers, they spent the next several days joining Washington, Comte de Rochambeau, the Marquis de Lafayette, and the other commanders in a series of comradely get-togethers in Williamsburg and its environs.

As Lafayette happily took part in those social occasions, including camp dinners, and basked in the victory, he also drew up a plan to re-engage the British. Under a plan approved by Washington, Lafayette would take his light infantry division, along with the Marquis de Saint-Simon's men, and meet up with General Nathanael Greene in Charleston in the event that the British resumed fighting. On October 21 and 22, Lafayette met with Rear Admiral Joseph Paul François de Grasse, asking him to transport those troops under Lafayette's command to North Carolina. But Grasse told Lafayette that he would not be able to help; he had orders to take his fleet to the West Indies where the French and Spanish were preparing to go on the offensive against the British.

Without Grasse's cooperation, the journey southward never happened. Lafayette instead remained at Yorktown until October 31, about the time the British fleet that Clinton had promised to send to Cornwallis reached the Chesapeake Bay—roughly two weeks too late. Grasse, as ordered, took off for the Caribbean on November 4.

❖

Instead of heading south, Lafayette left Virginia for Philadelphia with his brother-in-law—the Vicomte de Noailles—and other French officers on November 1, 1781. Lafayette received a hero's welcome in Baltimore, where he stopped en route, and in Philadelphia, where he held a series of meetings with members of the Continental Congress. He spent three weeks in Philadelphia, the national capital, presiding over the court-martial of John Moody and Lawrence Marr, two American Loyalist spies caught breaking into the State House in Philadelphia to steal congressional papers.

Before the trial ended, on November 23, Lafayette received his orders from Congress: he would return to France to work with Benjamin Franklin, John Adams, and John Jay "in accelerating the supplies which may be afforded by his Most Christian Majesty for the use of the United States."[2]

Lafayette and his entourage went to Boston, arriving during the first week of December. Again he was feted at dinners, receptions, and other gala get-togethers thrown in his honor. Congress, in its gratitude, provided Captain John Barry and his frigate the USS *Alliance*—the same ship that Lafayette had taken back to France in January 1779—to return him to his native land once again. The *Alliance* left Boston on December 23, 1781, and arrived at L'Orient on the southern Brittany coast on January 17, 1782. The young French general reached Paris four days later.

❖

The reception Lafayette received in France matched—if not exceeded—the rapturous welcomes he had received in Baltimore, Philadelphia, and Boston. "Our old warriors admire you; the young ones want to take you as a model," the Marquis de Ségur (the father of Lafayette's old army friend, the Comte de Ségur), who was now the minister of war, wrote to Lafayette.[3]

"Rejoicing," Foreign Minister Comte de Vergennes wrote to Lafayette from Versailles in December, "is very lively here and throughout the nation, and you may be assured that your name is venerated here. It is recognized with pleasure that although you did not have the lead in directing this large operation [at Yorktown], your prudent conduct and your preliminary maneuvers had prepared the way for its success."[4]

Lafayette received effusive greetings from virtually everyone in his home country: courtiers and ministers; artists and poets; pamphleteers, artists, and songwriters; and the common people in the street. Queen Marie Antoinette singled him out for praise, and her husband, King Louis XVI, promoted Lafayette to the rank of *maréchal de camp* (field marshal, the equivalent of either major or brigadier general) in the French Army, effective October 19, 1781, the day Cornwallis surrendered.

Louis XVI later presented Lafayette with the Cross of the Order of Saint Louis, the same high military honor his great-great-grandfather, the Comte de La Rivière, had received. His father-in-law, the Duc d'Ayen, also a recipient, had the honor of bestowing the cross on the young war hero.

With the promotion to *maréchal de camp,* the king and his advisers expected Lafayette to take part in the French war with the British. But Lafayette still considered himself a Continental Army soldier and wore his American uniform as he spent most of his time working with Franklin and company in their lobbying efforts to keep financial and material aid flowing from France to the United States. Lafayette also tried (without success) to help with the long, drawn-out peace treaty negotiations with England.

He and Adrienne enthusiastically took part in the rarified social life of the French court throughout 1782. That summer, the marquis purchased a lavish mansion on the Rue de Bourbon in Paris for 200,000 livres (around two million 2011 American dollars), and he spent an additional 150,000 livres restoring, remodeling, and furnishing the place. He hung a large portrait of George Washington in the drawing room. He and Adrienne moved in, and on September 17, shortly after her husband's twenty-fifth birthday, she gave birth to their third surviving child. The couple named their new daughter Marie-Antoinette-Virginie in honor of the French queen and Lafayette's adopted father's home state.

❖

Lafayette used his influence at court to have several French coastal cities named free ports for American shipping, which eliminated customs duties. And he continued his lobbying effort to have more French troops sent to the United States as the peace negotiations dragged on. The ministers balked at deploying additional troops, but in October, they assigned Lafayette to be the quartermaster general of a combined French-Spanish expeditionary force preparing to face off against the British, first in Gibraltar and then in Jamaica. The French and Spanish soon put together the largest armada ever assembled—sixty-six ships of the line and other vessels with a total of some 24,000 fighting men—off the southern Atlantic Ocean port city of Cadiz.

When the Comte d'Estaing, commander in chief of the operation, requested that Lafayette be put in charge of all the land forces, Vergennes agreed. And the ever-aggressive Lafayette convinced d'Estaing to add another part to the mission: after leaving the West Indies, they would sail to North America to finish off the British in the American South and in New York—and then force them out of Canada.

"My personal opinion is that a victory is needed before any treaty can be concluded," Lafayette wrote to Washington. "I will...keep my American uniform, and the outside as well as the inside of an American soldier. I will conduct matters and take commands as an officer borrowed from the United States...and will watch for the happy moment when I may join our beloved colours."[5]

The happy moment never came. Spurred mostly likely by the assembling of the massive French-Spanish armada, on January 20, 1783, the British signed preliminary articles of peace with the United States at Versailles. That agreement, among other things, included England's acknowledgment of the sovereignty and independence of the thirteen United States of America. It also officially ended the hostilities in North America. The French and Spanish promptly disbanded their huge armada.

"My own grand adventure seems to be settled, and America is sure of her independence," Lafayette wrote to his wife's aunt, the Comtesse de Tessé. "Humanity has won its case, and freedom will never again be without a refuge."[6]

❖

Lafayette wanted to convey the good news in person to his friends and colleagues in the Continental Congress. So he prevailed upon d'Estaing to allow him to sail back to America on the cutter *Triomphe.* But before the ship sailed, Lafayette returned for the first time in ten years to his childhood home, Chavaniac in Auvergne. During that time, Lafayette wrote a letter to Washington in which the young Frenchman for the first time spoke out against the institution of slavery. He proposed a plan that he said would be "greatly beneficial" to enslaved African Americans. The idea was that he and Washington would jointly purchase a "small estate" in which they would set up an experimental program for freed slaves, treating them "only as tenants." If that worked, Lafayette said, he wanted to spread the idea to the West Indies. "If it be a wild scheme," he told Washington, "I had rather be mad that way than to be thought wise on the other tack."[7]

Washington replied two months later. Near the end of a long letter, he addressed the issue. Washington, who owned more than 300 slaves, called the plan "a striking evidence of the benevolence of your heart" and said he would be "happy to join" Lafayette in "so laudable a work." But, Washington said, I "will defer going into a detail of the business, 'till I have the pleasure of seeing you."[8]

Washington never put such a plan into action, although he had positive words to say about the idea in a 1786 letter to Lafayette and in periodic communications with others in subsequent years. The Marquis and Adrienne de Lafayette became lifelong antislavery advocates, going so far as buying land in the French colony of Cayenne (now French Guiana) on the northern coast of South America to use as the same kind of program for freed slaves as he had proposed to Washington.[9]

When Lafayette's friend Henry Knox created the nation's first veterans' service organization, the Society of the Cincinnati, in May 1783, he enlisted Lafayette to certify which French officers would be eligible for membership. That—and Lafayette's strong and unequivocal opposition to slavery—clearly show that the once-precocious young marquis had matured into a respected international statesman. The Society of the Cincinnati—named after Lucius Quinctius Cincinnatus, the legendary Roman citizen-soldier—was designed to continue the camaraderie and friendships of allied officers after the war. It was open only to officers who fought in the Continental Army and Navy during the Revolution. Lafayette, Knox told him, would not need to be certified because "we consider you as an American and therefore one of us."[10]

When the American negotiating team of Benjamin Franklin, John Jay, and John Adams signed the final ten-article Treaty of Paris with

David Hartley (representing Great Britain) on September 3, 1783, Lafayette was with his wife and young family at their new home in Paris. The city celebrated the treaty, which brought the Revolutionary War to its final conclusion, officially confirmed Britain's recognition of American independence, and set the borders for the new nation.

The Marquis de Lafayette and his wife basked in the good feeling that the signing of the treaty engendered in Paris. They made their expansive new home into a popular salon in which visiting Americans, fellow French veterans of the American Revolution, and others interested in the ideas of republicanism flocked to discuss the issues of the day.

Outside the political realm, Lafayette carried on all-but-open extramarital affairs, including with two of the most beautiful women in France: Aglaé de Barbentane, the Comtesse d'Hunolstein, and Diane-Adélaide de Damas d'Antigny, known as Madame de Simiane—both of whom were married. The former broke off her affair with Lafayette after a year and gave up public life to live in a convent. Lafayette, however, continued his relationship with Madame de Simiane for many years.

❖

Lafayette sailed to America, accompanied by the Chevalier de Caraman, a French Army captain, for the third time on June 29, 1784, aboard *Le Courrier de l'Europe,* a French passenger ship. He landed in New York City—the first time he had set foot on Manhattan Island—on August 4, after a rough, five-week voyage. Lafayette stayed for more than four months, traveling to ten of the thirteen states and receiving rapturous greetings virtually everywhere he went. State and local governments, Revolutionary War veterans, and the citizenry at large honored him. The states of Maryland, Connecticut, and Virginia conferred honorary citizenship upon the marquis and his heirs.

James Madison, the future president who was between terms as a member of Congress, traveled with Lafayette for part of his trip through New York and New England. The young marquis and the French-speaking Virginian became close friends. "Wherever he passes," Madison wrote to Thomas Jefferson on September 7, "he receives the most flattering tokens of sincere affection from all ranks."[11] Lafayette also visited George Washington in retirement at Mount Vernon, where he stayed for ten days in August, and the two men had an emotional reunion.

Lafayette used his popularity and his wide circle of friendships with leading American politicians to his advantage as he traveled around the states backing the idea of a strong central government. At the time, the thirteen state governments acted all but independently and seriously disagreed on a wide range of issues, many of them involving boundaries and trade. Early in the trip, for example, on his way from New York to Virginia, Lafayette spoke to the Pennsylvania legislature, urging the lawmakers to support a strong federal union. Such a government was needed, Lafayette said, because it would support "the commercial wealth of America" and "will show to the greatest advantages the blessings of a free government."[12]

During his travels—accompanied by the Chevalier de Caraman; François de Barbé-Marbois, the French chargé d'affaires; and James Madison—Lafayette took time out to play a central role in negotiating a peace treaty with the Six (Indian) Nations at Fort Schuyler near the present-day city of Rome, in western New York.[13] He also had reunions with, among many others, Henry Knox and John Hancock in Boston at a boisterous celebration on October 19, the third anniversary of Cornwallis's surrender; Nathanael Greene in Providence, Rhode Island; Virginia Governor Patrick Henry during a lavish reception in Richmond (after stopping at Yorktown and Williamsburg) where he rejoined Washington; and many members of Congress in the new capital city of Trenton, New Jersey, including Richard Henry Lee, James Monroe, and Alexander Hamilton.

Lafayette gave a flowery address to Congress on December 11, in which he praised the nation's leaders and military men with whom he fought in the Revolution. Calling the United States "this immense temple of freedom," he expressed his wish that the country "ever stand a lesson to oppressors, an example to the oppressed, a sanctuary for the Rights of Mankind."[14]

He departed for France on the frigate *Nymphe* on December 21, 1784. As the French ship left New York Harbor, it fired off thirteen cannon shots and an American shore battery reciprocated. A little less than a month later, on January 20, 1785, Lafayette returned home to France once again, landing at Brest.

✥

Two days after Lafayette had landed in the United States the previous August, Thomas Jefferson had arrived in France to join Franklin and Adams as an American commissioner. After he returned to France, Lafayette forged a strong friendship with Jefferson, as the two men worked on common goals: to help the United States economically and to lobby for American interests in France, as well as in the rest of Europe. Lafayette sought out other Americans in Paris, and he and Adrienne made them welcome in their home, where—as they had done before he left for America—they hosted a weekly "American dinner."

Those occasions gave American officials and merchants the opportunity to meet with influential French officials and business-men where the lingua franca was English. Seventy-nine-year-old Benjamin Franklin regularly attended the dinners, as did Abigail and John Adams (before he became U.S. ambassador to England), and Thomas Jefferson, who took over as ambassador when Franklin went back to Philadelphia in May 1785. The oldest Lafayette children—Anastasie, seven, and Georges, five—were taught English in part so they could take part more fully in the weekly festivities.

Abigail Adams was one of many visitors impressed by the aristocratic family's openness and hospitality. "Immediately upon her coming into Paris, I called and paid my compliments to" Adrienne, John Adams's wife wrote in a December 1784 letter. "She is a very agreeable lady, and speaks English with tolerable ease.... The Marquise met me at the door, and with the freedom of an old acquaintance, and the rapture peculiar to the ladies of this nation, caught me by the hand and gave me a salute upon each cheek, most heartily rejoiced to see me. You would have supposed I had been some long absent friend, whom she dearly loved." [15]

◆

Lafayette broadened his commitment to civil liberties in 1785 by taking up the cause of Protestant freedom of religion in officially Catholic France. "Protestants in France are under intolerable despotism," Lafayette wrote to Washington in May.[16] Under French law, in fact, Protestants could not marry legally, their children had no legal rights, and their clergy were subject to prosecution.

During the summer of 1785, the twenty-seven-year-old Lafayette took up the invitation of seventy-three-year-old Frederick II (Frederick the Great) of Prussia to join him and other European generals for Prussian military maneuvers in what is now northeastern Germany. Lafayette spent three weeks at the Prussian court in Potsdam, enthusiastically taking part in balls, receptions, and other festivities. He used the occasion to extol the virtues of the new American nation to Frederick the Great—and to the other noblemen and Prussian officials he encountered—and to endorse the Prussian-American Treaty of Amity and Commerce, which Adams, Franklin, and Jefferson signed later that summer.

Around this time, Lafayette also visited Vienna, where he met with Emperor Joseph II of the Holy Roman Empire, the son of the Empress Maria Theresa and the brother of Marie Antoinette.

Lafayette discussed trade matters of the United States with the emperor and other high Holy Roman Empire officials. Lafayette continued lobbying for American interests when he returned to Paris.

Thomas Jefferson later said that Lafayette was by far the most dedicated and effective French advocate for the United States in France during Jefferson's term as U.S. ambassador, from May 1785 to September 1789. "When I was stationed in his country for the purpose of cementing its friendship with ours, and of advancing our mutual interests, this friend of both was my most powerful auxiliary and advocate," Jefferson said. "He made our cause his own, as in truth it was that of his native country also. His influence and connections there were great. All doors of all departments were open to him at all times. In truth, I only held the nail, he drove it."[17]

CHAPTER 11

The Most Dangerous
Man of Them All

Never has any man been placed in a more critical situation.

—Chevalier de La Luzerne, January 17, 1790[1]

THE MARQUIS DE LAFAYETTE SPENT A GOOD DEAL OF TIME IN 1786
and 1787 at the court of his longtime friend King Louis XVI. The
doomed French monarch presided over a bloated, fiscally strapped
feudal ship of state awash in self-serving aristocrats who enjoyed the
finest things in life as millions of commoners barely had the necessities of life. While dining at multi-course banquets and gaming at
the card tables at Versailles, Lafayette spoke to the king about social
reform, religious freedom, and his other socially progressive notions.
The king paid little heed to the idealistic hero of two worlds.

By early 1787, though, Louis XVI was forced to take action to try to deal with the consequences of his country's imminent bankruptcy. A significant part of the fiscal problem had been the result of the enormous outlays that went into supporting the Americans in their revolution against the British.

In February, at the urging of Minister of Finance Charles Alexandre, the Vicomte de Calonne, Louis XVI convened a legislative body known as the Assembly of Notables. It consisted of 144 appointed members of the upper classes, including seven princes, as well as magistrates and other government officials. The idea was to give the notables some legislative power while trying to institute a major change in the way the Crown did business—to wit, having the middle and upper classes pay taxes to the government for the first time.

Lafayette—somewhat surprisingly, given his well-known views on freedom and liberty—was included as a member of the Assembly, most likely because of his Noailles family connections. At twenty-nine, he was the unquestioned leader of the faction of nobles pushing for a form of constitutional monarchy—and the body's youngest member. Lafayette, as Horatio Gates put it, was an "old head upon young shoulders."[2]

Lafayette was there, as was Thomas Jefferson, when the king convened the Assembly of Notables on February 22, 1787, in a grand room at Versailles. Given the fact that its members came exclusively from the upper classes, it is not surprising that the notables turned down Calonne's taxation proposal. He soon resigned as the Assembly's president.

Also not surprisingly, Lafayette spoke out strongly in the Assembly for religious freedom for Protestants, for criminal law reforms, and against those in the upper classes who had accumulated wealth by exploiting the lower classes. Writing about the situation to John Adams in April, Lafayette said he was "a Republican in the heart" and "some seeds of liberty will be planted."[3]

He may have been planting some seeds of liberty, but the Assembly rebuffed Lafayette's proposals. He responded by offering a radical suggestion: convening a National Assembly—a legislative body that surely would usurp much of the king and nobility's authority and power. By taking the radical and rebellious stand of calling for a National Assembly in May 1787, Lafayette had become, in the words of Etienne-Charles Loménie de Brienne, the French cardinal who succeeded Calonne as president of the Assembly of Notables, "the most dangerous man of them all."[4]

The Assembly of Notables dissolved in late May. A National Assembly was not convened. At just about the same time across the Atlantic, the Constitutional Convention convened at the State House in Philadelphia to draw up what would become the document that has since become the foundation of the American government, the U.S. Constitution.

❖

In November 1787, King Louis XVI of France gave in to increasing pressure and granted some rights to his nation's Protestants, including allowing them to marry legally. That step, though, did nothing to help the Crown's fiscal situation. And with taxation reform dead, the French economy continued to sink in the summer and fall of 1787. With Lafayette continuing to speak out so strongly for reform—and not disguising his republican sympathies—the young marquis' close relationship with the king and queen began to crumble. The king stripped him of his *maréchal* rank, putting to an end—at least for the time being—Lafayette's French military career. Marie Antoinette banned Lafayette and his wife from attending royal dinners, dances, and other social occasions.

That fall, Lafayette was among a group of men who formed the Society of Thirty to debate how a new French National Assembly would be organized. The debate centered on how power would be apportioned among the nobility and those of lesser societal rank. Lafayette espoused a moderate position, in which he tried to balance his natural allegiance to the aristocracy with his strongly held ideas about freedom and equality. Those who agreed with him became known as "Fayettistes."

Instead of a National Assembly, Louis XVI decided to convene the Estates-General in September 1788. It would be the first time that the advisory body would be called into session in 174 years. Named after the three French "estates"—the clergy, the nobility, and nontitled citizens—the Estates-General would consist of 300 elected representatives from each of the three estates. This meant that the Third Estate—representing the citizenry at large (about 95 percent of the population)—would be institutionally outvoted by two to one.

When the Estates-General convened in Versailles on May 5, 1789, France had descended into a state of near anarchy. Severe food shortages led to near starvation in many places, which led to mob violence and food riots all over the country.

Lafayette won a seat in the Estates-General as a representative of his home in Auvergne, running on a platform that emphasized his support for an American-style form of republican government. Just a week earlier, on April 30, 1789, newly elected American President George Washington had delivered his first inaugural address before a joint session of Congress at Federal Hall in New York City, the new American capital.

The Estates-General was all but doomed from the start when the First and Second Estates (the clergy and nobility) voted to meet apart from the Third Estate. Because of that, Lafayette and others kept up the call to convene a National Assembly as tensions increased. On June 17, the Third Estate, joined by liberal-leaning nobles including Lafayette, declared itself to be the National Assembly. On June 20, with the Estates-General chamber in Versailles blocked by palace guards, the self-proclaimed National Assembly met at a nearby tennis court. They then took what became known as the Tennis Court Oath, vowing to take control of the nation's taxation system and pledging to continue meeting until a national constitution was drawn up.

During this tumultuous period, Lafayette finished writing his Declaration of the Rights of Man and of the Citizen. He had been working on the document for months, in consultation with Thomas Jefferson, among others. Modeled on both the American Declaration of Independence and on what would become the U.S. Bill of Rights, Lafayette's Declaration called for equality of all French people in the eyes of the law; guaranteed citizens the rights of "liberty, property, security, and resistance to oppression"; and called for freedom of speech, assembly, press, and religion.

❖

Louis XVI tried to dissolve what he viewed as an increasingly radical and republican National Assembly on June 23, but he backed down in the face of growing unrest among the citizenry. On June 27, 1789, he agreed to recognize the new National Assembly and ordered the nobility to join the body. On July 10, Lafayette officially introduced his Declaration of the Rights of Man in the National Assembly.

As news about the document spread quickly in Paris, orators took to street corners and pamphleteers distributed their incendiary work, firing up antiroyalist sentiment. Mobs formed; rioting and looting ensued. The situation became even more volatile the next day when Louis XVI fired his Swiss-born Finance Minister Jacques Necker for pushing him to give more power to the Third Estate in the Assembly. Then the king deployed troops in strategic areas around Paris and Versailles, further inciting the populace. Their pleas and taunts convinced many lower-ranking soldiers to join the protesting mobs in the streets.

On July 13, those renegade troops joined a crowd of some 40,000 in Paris that marched on the Hotel des Invalides, the huge military complex that also contained a hospital and veterans' retirement home. The mob forced its way through the gates and looted the place, taking away twenty cannons and some 28,000 rifles and bayonets. The armed throng then moved on the Bastille—a formidable, castle-like prison in the Marais District on Paris's Right Bank. At around 10:00 A.M. the next day, July 14, 1789, the mob stormed the Bastille, killing the loyal soldiers stationed there. Chaos and anarchy then spilled out onto the streets of Paris.

At this pivotal moment in French history, the National Assembly turned to the Marquis de Lafayette to try to restore order—or at least to try to prevent a full-scale violent revolution. On July 15, the governing committee of Paris asked Lafayette to take command of a police force of citizen-soldiers. Lafayette, never one to back away from a fight—much less pass up the opportunity to lead a small army—readily agreed.

He immediately assumed the post of commandant of the nascent militia, which he named the National Guard (*Garde Nationale*). Through the summer and into the fall, Lafayette, who turned thirty-two in September, put into practice his considerable military and political experience to organize the troops. The National Guard was charged with safeguarding the National Assembly (which moved to Versailles), as well as putting down revolutionary uprisings and mob violence, which flared up in Paris on an almost daily basis.

It was an unenviable job. Many royalists—including the king and queen—believed that Lafayette and his men were little more than revolutionaries. Conversely, many revolutionary leaders thought the marquis and his National Guard were doing the king's dirty work.

Lafayette stood undaunted. He threw himself into commanding the National Guard, concentrating at first on refashioning it into an effective peacekeeping force. Working tirelessly, he recruited many French veterans of the American Revolution and other regular military personnel. He secured thousands of flint-lock muskets for the men. The marquis integrated his professional soldiers with unpaid volunteers and organized them into battalions with responsibility for each of Paris's sixty districts. Lafayette made sure that the Guard's code included a provision that all officers would be elected by the rank and file. By mid-September, he had put together an effective military-police force of about 30,000 men.

He ordered that the Bastille—the symbol of the monarchy so despised by the citizens—be razed. When he later wrote to George Washington about the post–July 14 events, he enclosed the key to the Bastille's west portal in the letter. Lafayette sent the key to Washington via Thomas Paine, who was in London. Paine was thrilled with the entire exercise, which he saw as validating the cause of the American Revolution. "I feel myself happy in being the person through whom the Marquis has conveyed this early trophy of the spoils of despotism, and the first ripe fruits of American principles transplanted into Europe, to his master and patron," Paine wrote to George Washington on May 1, 1790.[5]

Always enamored of pomp, uniforms, and symbols, Lafayette used those devices to unify and strengthen his otherwise disparate group of National Guardsmen. Lafayette helped design a new uniform for his troops. It consisted of blue cutaway coats with white vests and leggings trimmed in red. He also encouraged each battalion to design its own unit flag. After outfitting the Guard in the new uniforms in early August 1789, Lafayette had the men take part in parades and other ceremonies on a regular basis to build morale and to show them off to the populace.

Lafayette also took the occasion to come up with a symbol that to this day represents France's national identity: the blue, white, and red tricolor. Looking for a new symbol that would help identify and unify the Guard, he added the symbolic color of the Royal House of Bourbon (white) to the red and blue colors of the city of Paris on the cockades (the knot of ribbons) that the National Guardsmen wore on their headgear. After Louis XVI gave the new tricolor cockade his blessing, it became the symbol of the nation, not just in Paris, but throughout all the French provinces. The blue, white, and red *tricolore* later became France's national flag.

❖

By the end of summer 1789, Lafayette and his National Guard had managed to bring some semblance of order to the center of Paris, but near anarchy reigned throughout most of the city and elsewhere in France. Rioters periodically raided government facilities and the homes of the nobility, summarily executing officials and aristocrats. For months at a time, Lafayette dealt almost every day with chaotic, hungry crowds on the streets. The mob distrusted anyone—including Lafayette—who represented authority and aristocracy. Lafayette used all of the skills he had learned on the field of battle and behind the scenes during the American Revolution to keep Paris from erupting into full-scale mob violence.

❖

As summer moved into fall, Lafayette continued to pour his seemingly endless energy into keeping law and order in Paris as the nation—he hoped—moved toward a constitutional monarchy. He regularly waded into crowds of angry demonstrators on his white horse, summoning his powers of persuasion to convince them that conditions would improve. The marquis reclaimed arms and ammunition that had been stolen from military storehouses. Lafayette arrested the most egregious perpetrators of violence. He also arranged to have shipments of wheat and flour brought to Paris from the provinces to try to address the acute shortage of bread.

He even enlisted his wife and daughter Anastasie in the effort. Adrienne and her daughter regularly accompanied Lafayette to National Guard reviews and other ceremonies. The Lafayette women also undertook charitable work, including taking up collections for the poor. Ten-year-old Georges Washington de Lafayette also got into the act, serving—at the behest of the National Guard and with his father's blessing—as an honorary second lieutenant of the Sorbonne district Guard unit.

Lafayette stepped into an enormous leadership void in Paris. In the summer and fall of 1789, he had become the most powerful man in the city—if not the nation. Working with the revolutionary government's mayor of Paris, Jean-Sylvain Bailly, Lafayette was, in essence, the city's chief judge, the head of the police, and the military governor.

He scored a political victory on August 26 when the National Assembly approved his Declaration of the Rights of Man, although it had been significantly amended. His proposal to ban slavery, for one thing, did not survive, but the provisions for freedom of religion and the press did.

✛

On October 2, 1789, Louis XVI rejected the National Assembly's Declaration of the Rights of Man. Two days later, Paris erupted in mob violence. Within hours, thousands of demonstrators, led by market women and fishwives (*les poissardes*), began an armed protest march on Versailles in a drenching rainstorm. Lafayette moved quickly, mobilizing his Guardsmen to try to control the mob on the twelve-mile march. He amassed some 15,000 troops and led the way out of Paris astride his white horse. When the crowd arrived at Versailles just after midnight, Lafayette, unarmed and with his uniform splattered with mud, met with the king in the royal apartments.

To do so, he had to endure the hostility of the royal household, including his own father-in-law, the Duc d'Ayen, the captain of the royal family's bodyguards who also was at the tense scene. Lafayette managed to convince the king that night to announce that he would take measures to feed the poor. That royal action calmed the crowd— for the moment.

But early the next morning, October 5, 1789, elements of the reagitated mob broke through the gates at Versailles. Lafayette charged into the maelstrom, sword in hand, and with his grenadiers managed to help save the royal family from all but certain execution. To try to calm the crowd, he made a show of presenting the king's Guards tricolor cockades, a symbol that the crowd cheered when the guards came out onto a balcony overlooking the Versailles courtyard. Acutely aware of symbolism, Lafayette then escorted King Louis XVI onto the balcony, where the momentarily satisfied crowd shouted, "*Vive le Roi!*" ("Long live the king!")

The mob then called for Marie Antoinette to show herself on the balcony, which she did, with her children in hand. The crowd shouted "No children!" and they were escorted back into the palace. When Marie Antoinette reappeared, Lafayette stood with her. Here's how the noted nineteenth-century British historian Thomas Carlyle described the scene in his famed history of the French Revolution: "Lafayette, with ready wit, in his high-flown chivalrous way, takes that fair queenly hand, and, reverently kneeling, kisses it: thereupon the people do shout *Vive la Reine*."[6]

◈

His acts quelled the mob's furor. Within hours, Lafayette organized a grand procession of some 60,000 to move out from Versailles on a journey to Paris. Contingents of National Guard troops led the march and brought up the rear. In the center, Lafayette escorted the royal family's carriage, along with Louis XVI's ministers, National Assembly deputies, and some 650 Versailles courtiers. Also in the crowd were soldiers and market women with wagons and carts filled with bread flour taken from the royal household.

When the procession reached Paris, Lafayette escorted the royal family to the all-but-abandoned Tuileries Palace, the former royal residence near the present-day Louvre Museum. His troops surrounded it, more to keep the royal family from fleeing than to protect them from the now-calm mob. Rumor had it that a plot was afoot in which Louis XVI, Marie Antoinette, and their children would escape to Austria, where they would come under the protection of the Queen's brother, Emperor Joseph II. The Holy Roman emperor, in fact, had massed troops on his domain's French borders—troops that included a large number of French nobles who had fled into solidly royalist Prussia, Austria, and elsewhere in Europe.

Lafayette himself had no plans to flee. He remained optimistic about the fate of his country—at least in public and in his letters to George Washington. "We have come thus far in the Revolution without breaking the ship either on the shoal of aristocracy, or that of faction," Lafayette wrote in January 1790, "and amidst the ever reviving efforts of the mourners and the ambitious we are stirring toward a tolerable conclusion."[7]

The Chevalier de La Luzerne—the former French minister to the United States during the American Revolution, now the French ambassador to England—summed up Lafayette's powerful yet precarious position in France as 1789 came to a close. Lafayette "finds himself at the head of the revolution....Never has any man been placed in a more critical situation."[8]

❖

This most critical situation continued unabated for Lafayette in 1790. Throughout that tumultuous year, the most radical revolutionaries gained more power and influence in the National Assembly and among the people. Three men led the radical faction: Maximilien Robespierre, an influential Assembly member who became president of the powerful and radical Jacobin Club; Georges-Jacques Danton, a fiery lawyer who had incited the crowds to storm the Bastille and march on Versailles, another Jacobin; and the journalist Jean-Paul Marat, the rabble-rousing editor of the journal *L'ami du People* (*Friend of the People*). Lafayette and his fellow moderates found it more and more difficult to make their voices heard.

An exception came on July 14, 1790, the first anniversary of the storming of the Bastille. An elaborate celebration called the Fête de la Fédération took place in Paris that day at the Champ de Mars, the large open space between L'École Militaire and the Seine River (the site today of the Eiffel Tower). Lafayette played a key role in orchestrating the event, which drew some 400,000 spectators. The *Times* of London called it a "grand spectacle of freedom,"[9] and the event turned out to be one of the largest public events in the history of Europe.

An army of workers labored for weeks to turn the open, empty field (which had been used by cadets at the L'École Militaire for drilling and parades) into a Roman-like amphitheater. They dug a pit some thirty feet deep. A tripled-arched Arc de Triomphe rose at one end of the field; an ornate "Altar of the Fatherland" dominated the center.

Some 50,000 National Guardsmen—along with officials from the city of Paris, National Assembly deputies, a children's battalion, French Army veterans, French Navy sailors and Army soldiers, provincial delegates, and others—marched eight abreast through the streets of Paris that rainy day. They arrived at the Champ de Mars at 1:00 P.M. to the booming of cannons and a roaring welcome from the multitudes. Charles Maurice de Talleyrand, the Bishop of Autun, began the ceremonies with a mass and benediction at the altar, surrounded by 300 priests wearing tricolor sashes over their vestments. After that, Lafayette took center stage.

At around 5:00 P.M., Lafayette took the oath to the principals of the new constitutional monarchy at the altar. Then he mounted his white horse and rode through the National Guardsmen's ranks to the pavilion that housed the royal family. Lafayette asked Louis XVI for permission to administer the oath to the troops, and then he did so with outstretched arms, finishing by placing his sword upon the altar. Following this, the king himself took the oath, swearing to uphold the decrees of the National Assembly.

"A respectful silence was succeeded by the cries, the shouts, the acclamations of the multitude," Helen Maria Williams, a young English poet who witnessed the spectacle, wrote in a letter. "They wept, they embraced each other, and then dispersed."[10]

The celebrations in the city went on for a week.

❖

When the festivities ended, however, the revolutionary unrest continued in France—as well as elsewhere in Europe. Antimonarchical rebellions of various magnitudes took place in Hungary, Poland, Sweden, Holland, and parts of what are now Germany and Italy. Royalists blamed Lafayette, among others, for spreading the tenets of republicanism. On the other hand, radical pamphleteers continued to accuse him of being a counterrevolutionary tool of the king.

"I am constantly attacked on both sides by the aristocratic and the factious party," Lafayette wrote to Washington in August 1790. "I have lately lost some of my favour with the mob, and displeased the frantic lovers of licentiousness, as I am bent on establishing a legal subordination."[11]

Lafayette also was very leery of a counterrevolution by royalists, abetted by monarchical governments outside France. The French royalists, Lafayette told Washington, "do what they can with all the crowned heads of Europe who hate us like the devil." Then there were the increasingly powerful Jacobins, who Lafayette said, "have divided the friends of liberty who accuse each other....I am endeavouring to bring about a reconciliation."[12]

There would be no reconciliation.

✠

On Easter Sunday, April 18, 1791, Louis XVI decided to take the royal family out of the Tuileries Palace to attend church services in the Paris suburb of St. Cloud. When National Guard troops, supported by throngs on the streets, stopped the royal carriage at the Tuileries gates, Lafayette tried to intervene. He ordered his men to allow the royal retinue to continue on their journey. But the National Guard continued to block the way, and Lafayette had little choice but to escort the family back into the palace.

Two days later, Lafayette decided to resign as commandant of the National Guard. But he changed his mind after his battalion commanders and Mayor Bailly came to his house, pledged their allegiance to him, and asked him to reconsider.

The attempted escape of the royal family that took place on June 20, 1791, did nothing to help restore order to the country. After the Easter incident, the family had assured Lafayette—the man primarily responsible for their well-being—that they would not leave the palace. But in mid-June, Lafayette and Bailly got wind that some kind of escape was planned.

They took "all possible precautions to prevent it," Earl Gower, the British ambassador in Paris, noted in a June 23 dispatch. Lafayette and Bailly, Gower said, "had both staid with his Majesty till one o'clock when they retired perfectly secure that no attempt of the sort could be made that night; having left a double guard and an extraordinary number of officers on duty against whom there is no suspicion of corruption."[13]

But sometime after 1:00 A.M. on June 20, Louis XVI, Marie Antoinette, and their children eluded their guards and stole off in disguise in a coach with a vague plan to start a counterrevolution in northeastern France. Lafayette learned of the escape at 5:00 A.M. He immediately dispatched National Guard troops to track down the family and bring them back to Paris.

Rumors spread that Lafayette engineered the escape. The most extreme radicals called for his arrest. On June 22, National Guard troops caught up with the king's carriage at Varennes, 150 miles from Paris. Lafayette rode out of the city to meet the troops escorting the royal family back to Paris. They felt the wrath of the mob all along the route. People lined the roads and jeered, with the most vicious taunts aimed at the hated queen.

When the entourage arrived in Paris, Lafayette and his National Guard succeeded in maintaining relative calm. He mollified the crowds by ordering that no one should bow or uncover their heads as the king's carriage rolled by, while also issuing orders strictly forbidding any violent demonstrations against the royal family. The official order reportedly said: "Whoever applauds the King will be flogged; whoever insults him will be hanged."[14]

Whether the National Guard commandant's order contained those exact words or not, it is emblematic of the conundrum in which Lafayette found himself as he tried to steer a middle path between the revolutionaries and the aristocracy as the French Revolution moved inexorably to its bloody conclusion.

CHAPTER 12

Poor Lafayette

I think the Army...will do pretty well.

—Marquis de Lafayette to George Washington, January 22, 1792[1]

WHEN THEY ARRIVED BACK AT THE TUILERIES PALACE, THE ROYAL FAMILY was placed under house arrest. King Louis XVI, Queen Marie Antoinette, and their children remained virtual prisoners there as conditions became more and more anarchic in Paris as spring moved into the summer of 1791.

On July 17, 1791, another noteworthy event took place at the Champ de Mars, but this time the Marquis de Lafayette was far from being the hero of the hour. The Jacobin Club held a large demonstration that day on the former drill field. The purpose was to build support for a petition drawn up by the radicals to declare France a republic and formally oust King Louis XVI.

Anticipating trouble, Lafayette had Paris mayor Jean-Sylvain Bailly declare martial law. Demonstrators flocked to the Champ de Mars by the tens of thousands. When the massive crowd grew disorderly, National Guardsmen under Lafayette's command waded in and dispersed them with little opposition. But later in the day, spurred on by Jacobin Georges-Jacques Danton and other extreme antimonarchists, more demonstrators appeared on the field. This time when Lafayette and his men tried to end the demonstration, some in the mob retaliated by throwing rocks at the Guardsmen. Lafayette's men then opened fire. As many as fifty people were killed in what became known as the Champ de Mars Massacre (*Fusillade du Champ de Mars*).

In the following days, the Jacobins attacked Lafayette even more viciously, vilifying him as a counterrevolutionary responsible for massacring innocent civilians. "Blood has just flowed on the field of the federation, staining the altar of the fatherland," the newspaper *Les Révolutions de Paris* thundered. When National Guardsmen "mowed many of them down, the crowd fled, leaving only a group of a hundred people at the altar itself. Alas! They paid dearly for their courage and blind trust in the law. Men, women, even a child were massacred there. Massacred on the altar of the fatherland."[2]

With the city under martial law, the National Guard cracked down on the radicals. Many fled Paris. Some were rounded up and executed. Those actions resulted in a state of relative calm in the city, allowing the National Assembly to reconvene in mid-September and complete its work on a written constitution. On October 1, France's first elected parliament, the 745-member Legislative Assembly (*Assemblée Législative*) convened.

Lafayette, believing that he had succeeded in his goal of helping bring a constitutional monarchy to his homeland, resigned as commandant of the National Guard. He promptly left Paris, returning to his home at Chavaniac in Auvergne. Mayor Bailly also resigned his post. In the November 16 election to choose his successor, a group of Fayettistes in Paris called upon the hero of two worlds to run for mayor. Lafayette agreed. He lost by a nearly two-to-one vote to Jérôme Pétion de Villeneuve, a lawyer and ardent antiroyalist politician who had played a leading role in bringing the royal family back from Varennes.

Leaving Paris in mid-October with his wife and family, Lafayette fully realized the fact that—ten years after the British surrender at Yorktown—he walked in the footsteps of his hero, George Washington, who had retired to Mount Vernon after the formal end of the American Revolution in 1783. He also well knew the similarities of his circumstances to those of Cincinnatus, the ancient Roman citizen-soldier who retired to his farm twice, after returning home victorious from the Roman wars.

Lafayette also was aware that although France may have been on the road to constitutional monarchy, the nation still faced extremely difficult political problems. That, he knew, had not been the situation in the United States when Washington retired to Mount Vernon.

The marquis thought about the differences between the United States in December 1783—when Washington left the army and retired to Mount Vernon—and France in October 1791, when Lafayette went home to Chavaniac. In a November 16 letter he wrote to William Short (Thomas Jefferson's successor as American ambassador), the marquis laid out these distinctions: "I have fought the same battles for the same cause with the same spirit and success at the head of the right angels against the wrong ones. But the scene of the one action was in Heaven, the other in Hell."[3]

Certainly things in France were hellish for Lafayette at this time. "Poor Lafayette," Gouverneur Morris, the French-speaking American statesman and businessman, wrote to Washington from Paris on October 22. "His enemies here are as virulent as ever.... He stands accused of designs, in conjunction with the dethroned monarch, to enslave his country." By resigning as head of the National Guard, Morris said, Lafayette "wounded the pride, insulted the feelings, and alarmed the fears of all France. And, by his thundering menaces to protect the royal family, he plunged them into the situation from which he meant to extricate them."[4]

The situation became increasingly dangerous not just for the royal family but also for other members of French society who had means—the upper and middle classes and the clergy—in late 1791 and early 1792. As inflation intensified and food shortages worsened, angry, hungry mobs vandalized chateaus, shops, and churches all over the country. Many aristocrats and their families left their homes and went into exile.

To add to the chaos, in November and December 1791 the Legislative Assembly, which the Jacobins controlled, pushed for war against Austria and Prussia. The revolutionaries wanted war primarily because they feared that the large number of French émigrés who had flocked to nearby Austrian territories would join with the Austrians and Prussians, invade France, and set in motion a counterrevolution.

❖

The king and his royalist supporters went along with talk of war, not to prevent counterrevolution but for the opposite reason: hoping that the Austrians and French exiles would prevail and defeat the French revolutionaries. In the midst of that roiling political atmosphere, the call went to Chavaniac in mid-December for Lafayette to return to military service and take command of one of three 50,000-man armies being formed to fight the Austrians. He complied willingly.

"I had refused every public emploïement that had been offered by the people, and still more had I denied my consent to my being appointed to any military command," Lafayette explained to Washington in a January 22 letter. "But when I saw our liberties and Constitution were seriously threatened and my services could be usefully emploïed in fighting for our old cause, I could no more resist the wishes of my country men, and as soon as the King's express reached my farm I sat out for Paris."[5]

Sixty-six-year-old General Rochambeau took command of the French Army of the North, which moved to the Belgian border; seventy-year-old Nicolas Luckner, the German-born French Army veteran, had the Army of the Rhine on the right. Lafayette was given command of the Army of the Center and set off to Metz to put together an effective fighting force.[6]

The marquis tried to meld National Guard forces and regular army troops into a cohesive fighting unit. It turned out to be a thankless task. For one thing, Lafayette received only about 25,000 troops, not the promised 50,000. And his supply situation was even worse than it had been during the American Revolution. He faced acute shortages of just about everything. Among other things, his army had no tents, and he had to requisition horses and carts from the populace.

Worse, Lafayette faced seemingly insurmountable discipline problems in the ranks, primarily from the many revolutionary sympathizers in the National Guard under the sway of the Jacobins. Many of his citizen-soldiers distrusted and hated their upper-class commanding officers, including their commanding general.

The army "is undisciplined to a degree you can hardly conceive," Morris wrote to Washington in late December. "Already great numbers desert." He called the National Guardsmen "corrupted scum" with "every vice and every disease which can render them the scourge of their friends and the scoff of their foes."[7]

Lafayette, at least in his letters to Washington, remained optimistic that he could overcome the serious discipline and supply problems. "I am going, and am the only one whose popularity can stand it, to establish, in spite of the Clubs and Jacobine clamours, a most severe discipline," Lafayette wrote to Washington in late January from Metz. "I think the Army afterwards will do pretty well."[8]

⬧

The French Army did far from well. Soon after the French Legislative Assembly voted on April 20, 1792, to declare war on Austria and Prussia, Rochambeau and Lafayette's armies moved toward the Belgian border. One of the first engagements in the war turned into a disaster. On April 29, at the Battle of Baisieux near Tournai in Belgium just over the French border from Lille, a 5,000-man French force under the Irish-born Count Théobald Dillon fought about 10,000 Austrian Army troops. Dillon had to retreat when he ran into a strong Austrian artillery barrage.

The retreat, at first orderly, turned into a panicked stampede made worse by violent confrontations between Dillon's cavalry officers and his men. Dillon escaped the chaos and took shelter in a farmhouse, only to be dragged out by his own men and taken to Lille. There he was "literally cut to pieces by an enraged populace and a worthless soldiery," according to his friend Gérard de Lally-Tollendal. "The Jacobins instantly denounced poor Dillon as a traitor, and the infuriated populace threw themselves upon him and hacked him to pieces," Lally wrote in a May 25 letter. "His aide-de-camp, Chaumont, a talented officer and a man of distinguished merit, shared his fate, while six Tyrolese prisoners were hanged by these wretches."[9]

Another stinging French defeat and retreat followed at Mons, Belgium. After that, more than a few commanders, including Rochambeau, decided they could not go to war with such an undisciplined army and resigned in disgust. Rochambeau was promptly arrested and imprisoned in Paris. Lafayette's brother-in-law, the Vicomte de Noailles, also resigned in protest. Noailles, Rochambeau's longtime aide and a strong supporter of Lafayette-like republican principles, fled to England.

❖

The ever-optimistic Lafayette did not consider resigning. He decided, instead, to try to take control of his undisciplined, undertrained, ill-supplied, and rebellious army. But before he did that on the Belgian border, Lafayette turned his attention back to Paris. He wrote to Mercy d'Argenteau, the Austrian ambassador to France, proposing a cease-fire so that he could return from the field with his troops to restore order and put an end to the rapidly growing rebellion against the king.

Lafayette's friends in the United States feared for his well-being. "I have not been a little anxious for your personal safety, and I have yet no grounds for removing that anxiety," George Washington wrote from Philadelphia on June 10.[10] Thomas Jefferson wrote to his French friend at about the same time, believing that Lafayette was in the field with a competent army about to take on the Austrians in a good cause—republicanism. "Behold you, then, my dear friend, at the head of a great army, establishing the liberties of your country against a foreign enemy," Jefferson wrote on June 16, 1792, from Philadelphia. "May heaven favor your cause, and make you the channel thro' which it may pour its favors."[11]

The same day that Jefferson penned that missive, Lafayette sent off a fiery letter from his headquarters in Maubeuge, France, near the Belgian border, to the Legislative Assembly. "It is not sufficient that this branch of the government should be freed from evil influence; the public weal is endangered; the fate of France rests mainly upon its representatives," Lafayette wrote. He went on to say that France faced two enemies, the Austrians and the radical revolutionaries in Paris. "You must destroy both," he told the Assembly. "Look around you. Can you not perceive that a faction, and, to avoid all vague allusion, I say, at once, the Jacobin faction, has been the cause of so many disorders! I openly charge this faction with these disorders!"[12]

Lafayette sent another letter that day, to Louis XVI, in which he pledged his allegiance to the king and said he would use military force against the rebels if it came to that. His letter to the Assembly suggested arresting the Jacobins on charges of high treason against the nation. If the Assembly didn't do so, Lafayette said, he would march his troops into Paris to take control of the situation.

It was an empty threat, and just about everyone in Paris knew it after the letter was read in the Assembly on June 18. It soon became painfully apparent that Lafayette had severely misjudged the situation. He either didn't realize or willfully disregarded three unassailable facts: the Jacobins were in firm control in Paris; the marquis had but tenuous control over his troops; and the king and his court were so cowed by the radicals that they also had turned against him.

The Jacobins' grip on Paris was especially apparent after June 20 when a huge crowd burst into the Tuileries, rushed into the king's apartments, and held him at gun and knifepoint for several hours until Mayor Pétion persuaded them to leave.[13] In the wake of that startling incident and Lafayette's intemperate letter, the Jacobins smelled blood and accused him of treason— and worse.

Gérard de Lally-Tollendal reported on what he encountered on June 21 among the crowds of people milling around outside the Tuileries Palace. "M. de Lafayette's letter had just been read to the Assembly," Lally wrote. "I heard from one, 'He is mad;' from another, 'He is a traitor; he is marching on us with his army;' a third affirmed that he was setting out for Coblentz. Women cried, 'He has betrayed our cause.' Men answered, 'He has adopted the tone of a dictator.'" Most people, Lally said, "pretended to believe that the letter was a forgery, and were for discovering the author and treating him as he deserved. Then they passed on to the king, and I heard them call this single-hearted, humane prince a rogue, a thief, and a murderer."[14]

The situation came to a head on June 28, 1792, when Lafayette arrived in Paris without his army to make a direct appeal to the Legislative Assembly. In another fiery declamation, he again called for the removal of the Jacobins and a return to the principles of constitutional monarchy. Many thought Lafayette was about to announce a military coup. The stage certainly was set for it. Instead, he stood all but powerless without his army, and the Assembly summarily turned down the former hero, accusing him of deserting his troops in the field.

It was a low moment in a life filled with highs. Lafayette had support among some like-minded nobles in the Assembly. But the radicals drowned out their voices. His June 28 speech did little more than add fuel to the already flaming Jacobin revolution. The speech "was very dangerous for the public liberty," wrote a twenty-two-year-old French artillery captain, who was in Paris at the time.[15] He said in a letter that Lafayette's appearance in the Assembly was a mistake. The artillery captain, Napoleon Bonaparte, would return to Paris in 1799 to lead a very successful military coup.

Even after his rude reception, Lafayette clung to the hope that his brand of constitutional monarchy would win out over the Jacobins. On June 29, he put out the word for volunteers from the National Guard to meet with him and a few of his fellow officers on the Champs Élysées in Paris where they would work on a plan to counteract the Jacobins. Lafayette expected thousands, but only about a hundred men showed up. Lafayette finally got the message. He left Paris on June 30. Jacobin leader Maximilien Robespierre called him a traitor to his country at a rally near the Palais-Royal after which a mob burned him in effigy.

❖

As the summer of 1792 wore on, things only got worse for Lafayette. "I verily believe that if M. de Lafayette were to appear just now in Paris unattended by his army, he would be torn to pieces," Gouverneur Morris—now the U.S. ambassador in Paris—wrote to Jefferson on August 1.[16]

Things were even worse for the royal family that summer. The catalyst that led to the final downfall of Louis XVI and the monarchy was the July 25 Brunswick Manifesto, issued by the Prussian Field Marshal Charles William Ferdinand, the Duke of Brunswick and commander in chief of the combined Austrian and Prussian armies. In it, the duke warned that Austria and Prussia would destroy Paris if the royal family were harmed. When the manifesto's contents reached the streets of Paris, the Jacobins' fury against the king hit a boiling point.

That anger peaked on August 10, 1792, when an enraged mob invaded the Tuileries Palace. As the crowds surged inside the gates, Louis XVI and Marie Antoinette fled by foot to the nearby Legislative Assembly where they were thrown into a small caged room. The mob then set upon the few remaining royal guards, slaughtered and dismembered them, and threw their body parts onto bonfires.

For three days, the mob held the king, queen, and their children captive in the small room, which previously had been used by reporters covering the Assembly. On August 13, the family was taken out, paraded through the streets, and imprisoned in a tower in the Temple, a twelfth-century fortress in an ancient district of Paris near the Bastille.

On August 11, the Assembly voted to bring to an end the reign of King Louis XVI—and to the constitutional monarchy that had gone into effect in the fall of 1791. A new ruling body, the National Convention, declared France a republic on September 21, 1792, officially abolishing the monarchy. Louis XVI went on trial for treason, was convicted, and executed by guillotine on January 21, 1793. Marie Antoinette had lost her head on October 16, 1792.

On August 14, 1792, the day after the royal family went to the prison in the Temple, Georges-Jacques Danton—the new minister of justice—put out an order for Lafayette's arrest. The marquis responded by trying to amass his troops to march on Paris. But he had lost the allegiance of nearly everyone under his command. Lafayette had two choices: to ride defiantly back to Paris to state his case once again and face certain imprisonment and execution, or to go into exile. He chose the latter.

The defeated Lafayette wrote to Adrienne on August 21, saying he had "been forced to flee into enemy territory from France," the nation he had "defended with so much love." Looking back on his role in the French Revolution, he told Adrienne that "with more ambition than moral sense, I could have had a very different existence." He went on to say that he would make his way to England, where he hoped the family would join him, and then they would settle in the United States. "Let us," he said, "establish ourselves in America, where we will find a liberty that no longer exists in France."[17]

Along with some fifty officers and men, including his longtime aide, the Chevalier de La Colombe, Lafayette rode across the French border in a driving rainstorm into Flanders, Belgium, in Austrian territory. But Lafayette never came close to escaping to England. Austrian troops soon took him and his men captive.

The marquis demanded that the Austrians allow him to contact British embassy officials so that he could go to England. His captors refused. Lafayette then fired off several letters demanding to be released, including one to the German Prince Albert of Saxony, the Duke of Teschen.

In an August 26 letter to William Short, the new U.S. ambassador to Holland, Lafayette complained that he and his men had been "detained by an Austrian detachment, which is absolutely contrary to the [rights of noncombatants]." He went on to ask Short to go to Brussels as soon as he received the letter and to insist that the Austrians permit a meeting.

"I am an American citizen," Lafayette told Short, "and an American officer. I am no longer in the service of France. In demanding my release, you will be acting within your rights."[18]

Lafayette soon would find out that his self-proclaimed status as an American officer carried no weight whatsoever with his captors.

CHAPTER 13

Companions of Misfortune

I can neither approve of an arbitrary government, nor associate myself with it.

—Marquis de Lafayette, March 1800[1]

NOT LONG AFTER THE AUSTRIANS TOOK THE MARQUIS DE LAFAYETTE
and his comrades prisoner, all hell broke loose in France. It began
after radical revolutionaries spread rumors that the Austrians and
Prussians were heading toward Paris to mount a counterrevolution
with the help of French royalists. That led to enraged mobs going on
a six-day rampage in Paris beginning on September 2, 1792. In what
became known as the September Massacres, angry crowds slaughtered
more than a thousand people—men, women, and children—who
they believed would be joining the counterrevolution.

"The unhappy victims were butchered like sheep at a slaughter house," the *Times* of London reported on September 10. The "trunkless heads and mangled bodies were carried about the streets on pikes in regular cavalcade. At the *Palais Royal*, the procession stopped, and these lifeless victims were made the mockery of the mob.... The mangled bodies of others are piled against the houses in the streets.... The carcasses lie scattered in hundreds, diffusing pestilence all around."[2]

The antiroyalist mayhem spread throughout the country during this period of the French Revolution, which came to be known as "The Terror," or "The Reign of Terror." Later in September and throughout the fall of 1792, the Jacobins seized the possessions of suspected counterrevolutionaries all over the country. That included Lafayette's Chavaniac and all of his other estates and holdings. Jacobin thugs threatened Adrienne de Lafayette, who was living in Chavaniac with their children and with Lafayette's aged aunt, but allowed the family to stay in the house—for the time being.

❖

Lafayette and his family, again, found themselves under attack from both sides in the Revolution. The Jacobins terrorized his family in France. His captors treated him as though he were an ally of the French revolutionaries. King Frederick William II of Prussia, in fact, ordered Lafayette imprisoned indefinitely for fomenting revolution.

On September 18, Lafayette and three other French officers were thrown into a fetid dungeon in Wesel, a Rhine River city in what is now northwestern Germany north of Dusseldorf. The Frenchmen were held in separate, rat-infested cells containing little more than wooden boards for beds. The food was slop; the guards were sadistic.

"The treatment of M. de la Fayette and his companions of misfortune at Wesel is cruel and rigourous in the extreme," U.S. ambassador to Holland William Short wrote to Gouverneur Morris. "It is certain," Short said, "that he is the individual of all of France that both the Austrians and Prussians hate the most.... The desire of revenge and determination to punish made them commit the most flagrant act of injustice."[3]

It was little consolation to Lafayette that the peasant-fueled French military won a significant victory on September 20 in Valmy in northwestern France. That day, the French Army of the North under Charles François Dumouriez and François Christophe Kellermann's Army of the Center soundly defeated the Duke of Brunswick's combined Austrian, Prussian, and French émigré forces. Nor did Lafayette take any measure of comfort in the fact that that engagement turned the tide of the war. Eventually, the French Army and Navy went on to take significant amounts of territory from the Austrians and Prussians.

✤

Early in December 1792, Jacobin leader Maximilien Robespierre put out an official order condemning Lafayette to death for crimes against the French people. Soon thereafter, the marquis' captors took him and his fellow ill-treated prisoners farther east to the city of Magdeburg in present-day Germany. Again, Lafayette suffered greatly in a dank dungeon, deprived of light, edible food, and anything resembling decent sanitary conditions.

As the war raged in Europe during the first months of 1793, George Washington, about to begin his second term as president, declared American neutrality. His new nation was in no position fiscally—nor was it inclined—to come to the aid of the French in their Revolution. Any sentiment for aiding the French evaporated following Louis XVI's beheading and the Reign of Terror under Robespierre and his ruling clique, the Committee of Public Safety, that enveloped France in full force in the fall of 1793. Thousands of counterrevolutionaries, members of other political parties, priests, and aristocrats were executed after being accused of working against the Revolution and in the name of preserving the revolutionary republic.

During the Terror, Washington and Lafayette's other American friends did what they could to help the marquis and his family. Washington and Morris, for example, had funds sent to Adrienne. The Terror, which would last until late July 1794—ending only after Robespierre himself was beheaded—had a devastating impact on the Lafayette and Noailles families. In September, a Jacobin mob ransacked Chavaniac and carted Adrienne, her eldest daughter Anastasie, and Lafayette's seventy-three-year-old Aunt Charlotte off to a nearby prison. They later were returned to Chavaniac, but put under house arrest. On October 8, 1793, Adrienne's grandmother, mother, and sister Louise, who were in Paris caring for her aged grandfather, also were placed under house arrest.

Early in 1794, the Austrian military shipped Lafayette and his fellow French prisoners to another dank prison, this one in the Prussian city of Neisse, west of Magdeburg. A few months later, the prisoners were taken to yet another dungeon in the Bohemian city of Olmütz (now known as Olomouc in the eastern part of the Czech Republic).

In November 1793, Jacobin agents had taken Adrienne from Chavaniac and imprisoned her in nearby Brioude. Six months later, in the spring of 1794, she was transferred to Paris and imprisoned at the Hotel de La Force, a former grand Parisian mansion. Sixteen-year-old Anastasie, who was not arrested, made her way to Paris to try to win her mother's release. She had no success. But the U.S. ambassador, Gouverneur Morris, convinced Robespierre that guillotining Adrienne would do France's cause no good in America, where the Lafayette name was revered. She remained in prison but was taken off the official execution list. Her grandmother, mother, and sister Louise were not so fortunate; they were publicly guillotined on July 22, 1794.

Adrienne was later put into another makeshift Parisian prison at Collège du Plessis, her husband's first school. She was freed on

January 22, 1795, mainly through the efforts of Lafayette's old friend James Monroe of Virginia, who had succeeded Gouverneur Morris as U.S. ambassador to France.

Monroe also arranged for fifteen-year-old Georges Washington de Lafayette to escape the Revolution and go to the United States soon after his mother's release. And in September 1795 he helped arrange passage for Adrienne and the two Lafayette daughters, Anastasie and Virginie, to Vienna. They traveled under American passports issued to the Motier family of Hartford, Connecticut.[4] On October 3, 1795, Adrienne met in Vienna with Emperor Francis II, who gave her permission to join her husband in his jail cell at Olmütz. Within weeks, the three Lafayette women had an emotional reunion with the marquis in his prison cell. The four family members stayed in that prison together for two more years.

Although the family's plight brought sympathy and support from influential figures in Europe and America, conditions in the prison remained brutal. Adrienne's health suffered the most. When the Austrians finally released the family on September 19, 1797 (thirteen days after Lafayette's fortieth birthday), Adrienne suffered from a variety of serious ailments. Lafayette cited her precarious health as the reason he turned down an invitation from George Washington to immigrate to the United States.

"My own health, altho' it is impaired could, I think, tolerably support a voyage" across the Atlantic, Lafayette wrote to Washington early in October 1797. "My daughters are not ill. But Mrs. Lafayette's sufferings in this cruel unhealthy captivity have had such a deplorable effect upon her that in the opinion of every physician, and every man of sense, it would be an act of madness to let her embark in this advanced season of the year."[5]

The Austrians freed the Lafayette family with the proviso that they leave immediately and forever. At home, the French government—now organized under a system called the Directory—let Lafayette know that they would allow him back into the country but only if he took an oath in support of that government, which had taken power two years earlier. Lafayette refused because, he said, the Directory came to power illegally and unconstitutionally. In response, Foreign Minister Charles Maurice de Talleyrand ordered all of Lafayette's lands seized and sold.

Lafayette now had almost no resources, but he had his wife's family. He, Adrienne, and their daughters reunited with Adrienne's sister Pauline and her husband in Denmark, where they moved into a small, Noailles-family castle. Georges Washington de Lafayette returned from America and joined them there in January of 1798.

It appeared that the family would soon resettle in the United States. But the XYZ Affair—a scandal involving three French government officials who demanded bribes from American diplomats—all but froze relations between the two former allies. That fiasco ended any possibility that the French government would permit the Lafayettes to emigrate.

Late the following year in 1799, Lafayette reluctantly pledged his support to France's new leader, the wildly popular Napoleon Bonaparte, who had led a coup in November and became first consul. Napoleon allowed Lafayette to return to France only if he pledged to refrain from taking part in any political activity. Lafayette, urged on by Adrienne, who had intervened directly with Napoleon, agreed. The family moved to one of the lesser Noailles mansions, the Chateau de La Grange, in Brie, about forty miles outside of Paris.

It was while he was at La Grange in February 1800 that Lafayette learned of George Washington's death on December 14, 1799. The French government did not allow him to attend the funeral ceremony that Napoleon arranged to honor Washington on February 8 at Les Invalides in Paris.

On March 1, 1800, Napoleon restored Lafayette's French citizenship. Later that year, the marquis paid a visit to his elderly aunt in

Chavaniac for the first time in nine years. Napoleon's government offered Lafayette several top-level jobs, reportedly including ambassador to the United States, as well as membership in the French Legion of Honor. He refused them all for the same reasons he had turned down the Directory's offer to pledge allegiance to that government: to protest an autocratic and unconstitutional French regime.

"If Bonaparte had been willing to serve the cause of liberty, I should have been devoted to him," Lafayette wrote in his memoirs. "But I can neither approve of an arbitrary government, nor associate myself with it."[6]

The government became even more autocratic in 1802 when an adoring French populace voted Napoleon, fresh from his military victories throughout Europe, consul for life. Two years later, in May 1804, another plebiscite endorsed Napoleon's creation of the French Empire. On December 2, the conquering military hero crowned himself Napoleon I, emperor of the French, at Notre Dame Cathedral in Paris.

❖

Lafayette spent much of his time during Napoleon's reign at La Grange as a gentleman farmer. He remained there after Adrienne died on December 24, 1807, at age forty-eight, from complications arising from the myriad maladies she incurred during her incarceration.

Before and after his wife's death, Lafayette received a stream of adoring visitors, including many Americans. But he stayed on the political sidelines, even though rumors repeatedly circulated that Lafayette was plotting to overthrow Napoleon. Although there is no evidence that Lafayette did anything even remotely subversive, Napoleon believed he was a threat to his regime. "Everybody is cured of his errors except Lafayette," Napoleon said. "You see him there in tranquility. . . . I tell you, he is ready to begin again."[7]

But Lafayette stayed away from the national political stage. He played no role when Paris fell to the British in the spring of 1814 and Napoleon abdicated and went into exile in Elba. And the marquis continued to stay on the sidelines when Louis XVI's brother, the Comte de Provence, restored Bourbon rule as King Louis XVIII in April 1814.

However, in March 1815, when Napoleon returned from exile, Louis XVIII fled, and Napoleon launched his short-lived second reign, Lafayette himself returned to national politics. In May, he won a seat in the French Chamber of Deputies from Brie. Once in office, Lafayette began to speak out loudly against Napoleon and in favor of a constitutional monarchy. After the June 18, 1815, defeat at Waterloo, Lafayette led the call in the Chamber for Napoleon's abdication, which came to pass, and for the National Guard to be reformed, which did not. He also pushed to have the liberal-leaning Louis-Philippe, the Duke of Orléans, reclaim the French throne, rather than have the autocratic Louis XVIII reinstated, but was unsuccessful.

During the Second Restoration of Louis XVIII, the Marquis de Lafayette, in his position as a leading liberal in the Chamber of Deputies, spoke out constantly for the principles he had long espoused: constitutional government with freedom of the press and civil liberties—not just in France, but throughout the world. He supported revolutionary movements in Italy, Greece, Spain, Portugal, Brazil, and elsewhere. The repressive government of Louis XVIII despised him, especially after a failed 1821 coup, which Lafayette tacitly supported. Then, in what most likely was a rigged election, Lafayette lost his seat in the Chamber of Deputies in 1823.

◈

In 1824, Lafayette, now in his sixty-seventh year, accepted an invitation from the U.S. Congress and his old comrade and friend

President James Monroe to visit the United States. Congress voted unanimously to invite Lafayette back to America and to transport him on a U.S. warship. Lafayette chose instead to book passage on the American merchant ship *Cadmus,* which left Le Havre, France, on July 13, 1824. Lafayette made the trip with his son Georges, a valet, and Auguste Levasseur, his secretary. Levasseur would keep (and publish) a detailed account of the visit and send reports back home to French newspapers.

The ship sailed into New York Harbor on August 15. As the *Cadmus* approached Staten Island, "its inhabitants, [in] the expectation of some great event...in all haste [ran] to the shore," Levasseur wrote. As cannons thundered from the aptly named Fort Lafayette, "the report of Lafayette's arrival was quickly spread over the great city of New York, and the bay was already covered with boats conveying crowds of citizens, who hastened to Staten Island to give him the first salutation, that welcome, which the whole nation afterwards repeated with so much enthusiasm."[8]

The whole nation did seemingly spill over with gusto for the Marquis de Lafayette throughout his thirteen-month, 6,000-mile visit to all twenty-four American states. In city after city and state after state, he received raucous, highly charged hero's welcomes as tens of thousands lined roads and city streets, shouted his name, and sang his praises at banquets, breakfasts, dinners, receptions, and balls. Governors greeted him effusively in their state capitals. The marquis' fellow Masons put on banquets for him virtually everywhere he traveled, as did his fellow Society of the Cincinnatians. Lafayette enthusiastically embraced the adulation everywhere he went. He was especially moved when reuniting with former Revolutionary War comrades and fellow veterans.

He spent two weeks in Boston, where he met with John Adams and took part in fiftieth-anniversary commemorations of the Battle of Bunker Hill in June 1825. Lafayette made two visits to the Brandywine battlefield. He paid his respects at Mount Vernon. The

Frenchman also took part in ceremonies at Yorktown on October 19, the anniversary of General Cornwallis's surrender. He met with Andrew Jackson in Nashville. Lafayette also spent a month in the White House as the guest of newly elected President John Quincy Adams. Lafayette's December 10, 1824, speech in the U.S. House of Representatives marked the first time that a foreign dignitary addressed that body.[9] He visited Charleston, New Orleans, St. Louis, Baltimore, and Philadelphia, among other places. Everywhere he went, Lafayette proclaimed his love for the United States and the republican ideals for which it stood.

Among the many highlights of the trip was a poignant visit in November 1824 to an ailing Thomas Jefferson at his Virginia mountaintop home, Monticello. Lafayette and his entourage, which included the Richmond volunteer cavalry, arrived in Charlottesville on November 4, after visits to Petersburg and Richmond. The town fathers declared the day a holiday—as many others cities and towns did throughout Lafayette's trip.

Jefferson sent a carriage drawn by four gray horses into the nearby town to bring Lafayette up to Monticello. The carriage made the short trip up the small mountain in a long procession, which included the cavalry detachment. When the party arrived atop the mountain, a bugle sounded, and hundreds of spectators, including James and Dolley Madison, formed a semicircle in front of the house.

"The carriages drew up in front of the building," the Charlottesville *Central Gazette* reported. "As soon as the General drove up, Mr. Jefferson advanced to meet him, with feeble steps; but as he approached, his feelings seemed to triumph over the infirmities of age, and as the General descended they hastened into each other's arms. They embraced, again and again; tears were shed by both, and the broken expression of 'God bless you General,' 'Bless you my dear Jefferson' was all that interrupted the impressive silence of the scene, except the audible sobs of many whose emotion could not be suppressed."[10] Lafayette and his party spent ten days enjoying Jefferson's hospitality and being feted at the University of Virginia.

In December 1824, Congress, at President Monroe's request, voted to bestow $200,000 on Lafayette—the equivalent of about $2 million today—in compensation for what he did for the United States during the American Revolution. Some members objected to the large outlay, but the overwhelming majority agreed with Rep. Charles Fenton Mercer of Virginia, who said that Lafayette's "services to our cause—the cause of freedom in Europe and in America" were "immeasurable." There "is not a man who now, or may hereafter tread our soil or breathe our air," Mercer said, "who is not, or will not owe him an inestimable debt—a debt to be felt, not to be computed."[11]

Lafayette left the United States for the last time on September 8, 1825, two days after his sixty-eighth birthday. He and his entourage—which included a military officer from each of the twenty-four states—boarded the aptly named steamboat *Mount Vernon* on the Potomac River in Washington D.C. The ship sailed down the river to St. Mary's in southern Maryland where Lafayette and company transferred to a larger ship for the Atlantic crossing. This time, Lafayette accepted the Americans' offer for passage on a U.S. warship, the newly commissioned forty-four-gun *Susquehanna,* which the navy renamed *Brandywine* in Lafayette's honor.

Lafayette took a special memento with him on the *Brandywine:* a large trunk filled with American soil, which he said he wanted to be placed on his grave.

CHAPTER 14

The Prime Mover

[Louis-Philippe] will be the instrument of a free people, subordinate to those principles of civil and religious liberty, whose greatest champion you have been.

—President Andrew Jackson to Lafayette, July 1830[1]

THE MARQUIS DE LAFAYETTE'S VOYAGE BACK TO FRANCE WAS NOT AN easy one. Storms buffeted the *Brandywine* for a good part of the three-week trip. Lafayette, a veteran of rocky Atlantic crossings, arrived back home in good health and spirits. Upon his return, the marquis learned that Louis XVIII had died at age sixty-nine in Paris on September 16, 1825, while Lafayette was at sea. Sixty-six-year-old Charles X, the former Comte d'Artois whom Lafayette had known from boyhood when they were both students at the riding academy in Versailles, succeeded his older brother. Charles X, an ultraroyalist, had gone into exile in England when the French Revolution broke out in 1789. He had returned to France in 1814.

The French people welcomed the new king. But the reception did not last very long. Within a year, Charles X instituted a series of authoritarian measures that did not sit well with many Frenchmen, including those committed to the ideals of constitutional monarchy. Lafayette was the nation's most respected, well-known, and outspoken member of this opposing group.

In 1827, Lafayette stepped back into the national political arena in his seventieth year, easily winning a seat once again to the Chamber of Deputies. Lafayette used that position to carry on his life's work: speaking out loudly and passionately against repressive government and for the ideals of democracy and freedom. Charles X, unhappy with the election results that brought a large number of liberals into the Chamber, dissolved the body and called for new elections. Lafayette and the other liberals overcame the Crown's attempt at ballot stuffing and won back their seats.

The Marquis de Lafayette continued to speak out in fiery speeches against the excesses of Charles X, advocating for American-style representative government in the Chamber. He also did so at social gatherings at Chateau de La Grange, where he held court for many Americans and others who came there to pay their respects and hear him expound on his political views.

This activity did not go unnoticed. Government agents continually spied on Lafayette. One government report commented on the "troublemaker…and his seditions toasts…in honor of American liberty."[2] Lafayette's reputation and popularity, however, prevented the king from taking any action against the marquis, other than keeping a close eye on him.

Between 1827 and 1830, the king instituted more repressive measures, including press censorship. The spark that set off the July

Revolution of 1830 came when Charles X signed a series of decrees on July 25. Known as the Ordinances of Saint-Cloud, the decrees instituted even tighter press censorship, dissolved the Chamber of Deputies, and changed the electoral laws to take away the middle class's right to vote. What ensued was the three-day July Revolution, which ended in Charles X's exile and his cousin Louis-Philippe, the Duke of Orléans, taking over as the new constitutional monarch of France.

The July Revolution marked the end of the reign of the royal House of Bourbon and the rise of the House of Orléans. The Marquis de Lafayette once again played a central role in a momentous, regime-changing revolution—this one a comparatively little-known but important event in French history.

Le Moniteur, a royalist newspaper, published the Ordinances of Saint-Cloud on July 26. The revolution began the next day, July 27, when massive numbers of citizens—liberals, workers, students, shop-keepers, and others—took to the barricades in the streets of Paris. Liberal and radical newspapers defiantly put out editions despite a government ban to shut down, contributing to the atmosphere of rebellion.

Early that very warm evening, French troops and revolutionaries faced off against each other in the streets of Paris. The mob pelted the soldiers with rocks and other improvised missiles. The troops fired back. By daybreak, some twenty-one civilians lay dead. The fighting continued sporadically the next day, July 28, when the leaders of the revolt demanded that Charles X—who had hunkered down at Saint-Cloud in Paris's far western suburbs—revoke the hated ordinances. The king and his ministers refused.

On July 29, the third and final day of the revolution, the French troops wilted in scorchingly hot conditions. That allowed the revolutionaries to take control of the streets of Paris. All over the city, people tore down white-and-gold House of Bourbon flags and replaced them with the blue, white, and red tricolor.

Early that afternoon, mobs stormed the Tuileries Palace and occupied the building as the royal guards deserted their posts. A near riot ensued, along with some looting. Before the afternoon ended, revolutionaries took over the greatest prize, the Hôtel de Ville (City Hall), and liberal members of the Chamber of Deputies began setting up a new constitutional monarchy.

Lafayette joined the other deputies at the Hôtel de Ville to take part in the transition. Nearly everyone agreed that Lafayette should reprise his 1789 role and take over the National Guard. The stage also was set for Lafayette—as it had been in 1792—to stage a coup and take control of the nation.

The marquis enjoyed wide popularity as the most important and famous living Frenchman who had played a major role in the 1789 Revolution. As Odilon Barrot, a liberal member of the Chamber, put it: Lafayette was "for the nation, and particularly for the people of Paris, the personification, the living expression, of what had been great and legitimate in the Revolution of 1789."[3] What's more, with Charles X all but crippled politically, a gaping power vacuum existed, and more than a few members of the Chamber of Deputies asked Lafayette to assume power.

But Lafayette stood by his republican principles and agreed only to take over the National Guard. His only goal, he said, was to restore order and usher in a smooth transition to constitutional monarchy under fifty-six-year-old Louis-Philippe, who had supported the 1789 French Revolution but had fled to England and the United States after the radicals took over.

❖

Reconstituting the National Guard proved to be a difficult, multi-faceted task. Lafayette, now nearly seventy-three years old, proved to be up to it. "He was occupied with the organization of the legions, with the reception of deputations from Paris and the departments," the physician, National Guard surgeon, and Lafayette admirer Jules Cloquet later wrote. "He read applications and listened to claims addressed to him, arranged disputed questions, drew up nominations, visited the wounded in the hospitals, frequently mounted his horse, and endured the fatigues of the protracted reviews of the National Guards. In short, he did every thing, and without injury to his health. His strength seemed absolutely to increase with the multiplied nature of his duties."[4]

On July 31, with Lafayette in control of the National Guard and the guardsmen in control of Paris's streets, eighty-nine members of the Chamber of Deputies issued a proclamation ending the reign of the despised Charles X. The proclamation invited the Duke of Orléans, "a Frenchman who has never fought except for France," to "exercise the functions of Lieutenant-General of the Kingdom."[5]

Louis-Philippe had arrived in Paris on July 30, taking up residence at the longtime Orléans family mansion, the Palais-Royal. He made his way the next day on horseback—rather than a royal coach—through the still-barricaded streets to the Hôtel de Ville.

"I am simply an old National Guardsman come to visit his former general," the duke said as he walked into the building to greet Lafayette.[6] He did so to a less-than-welcoming reception, at least by the people in the streets. Eyewitnesses said that there were more shouts of "*Vive la liberté*"[7] and "*Vive Lafayette*" than "*Vive le Duc d'Orléans.*"

With this dramatic meeting of the duke and the marquis, Lafayette once again stepped in to play a key role at a crucial moment in French history. His support would smooth the way for Louis-Philippe to take over the nation; his opposition would make it all but impossible.

"Every one awaited with impatience the reception which Lafayette would give to [Louis-Philippe]," Bernard Sarrans, Lafayette's aide-de-camp who was on the scene, later wrote. "All eyes were fixed on these two personages.... When Lafayette, extending his hand to the Duke of Orléans, presented him with a tri-colored flag, and led him to one of the windows of the Hôtel de Ville, the enthusiasm of the people burst forth, and more frequent cries of *Vive le Duc d'Orléans!* were mingled with the universal shouts of *Vive Lafayette!*"[8]

"At the apparition of the Duc d'Orléans and Lafayette, both enfolded so to speak in the tricolour," Odilon Barrot—who also was there—said, the July Revolution "was terminated. The Duc d'Orléans had entered the Hôtel de Ville a simple pretender; he might have found his death there. He left it, carrying the noblest crown in the world, and proclaimed by the people of Paris."[9]

Still, a significant number of deputies were not completely convinced that Louis-Philippe would be the constitutional monarch they envisioned. Lafayette's unequivocal support of the duke, however, ended all doubt among the deputies—and the crowds outside.

"Lafayette now interposed his all-powerful authority with the chiefs of the insurrection, and obtained from them a promise that tranquility should not be disturbed," Sarrans said, "pledging himself, on his part, to obtain from [Louis-Philippe] those guarantees which the revolution had a right to exact, and which he summed up in the words, 'a popular throne, surrounded by republican institutions.'"[10]

According to Sarrans, the following conversation took place between Lafayette and the duke:

"You know that I am a republican, and that I consider the Constitution of the United States as the most perfect system that has ever existed," Lafayette said.

"I think so, too," Louis-Philippe replied. "It is impossible to have lived two years in America without being of that opinion. But do you think, in the situation in which France stands, and in the present state of public opinion, we can venture to adopt it here?"

"No," Lafayette replied. "What the French people want at the present juncture is a popular throne, surrounded by republican institutions."

"That is just what I think," the duke said.[11]

On July 31, 1830, the day that Charles X fled Versailles, the Duke of Orléans accepted the throne with Lafayette's ringing endorsement. The new ruler let it be known that he would not be the "king of France," but rather Louis-Philippe I, the "king of the French."

Three days later, on August 3, Charles X signed his official letter of abdication. Louis-Philippe—the "citizen-king" who disdained wearing traditional royal robes and lived in the Palais-Royal rather than the more-opulent Tuileries Palace—took the oath of office as king of the French on August 9.

Charles X left France on August 16 and went into exile in England. Sarrans reported that the last words the deposed king uttered to his escort before boarding his ship to England were: "The old republican Lafayette has been the prime mover of all this mischief."[12]

The result of the July Revolution went over well in the United States. President Andrew Jackson wrote to Lafayette, saying the hero of two worlds was "right in calling the Duc of Orleans to the throne—he will be the instrument of a free people, subordinate to those principles of civil and religious liberty, whose greatest champion you have been."[13]

Those words proved not to be prophetic. Within months, the Chamber of Deputies turned more conservative. In late December, Louis-Philippe did not stand in the way when the Chamber abolished the position of National Guard commander—a slap in the face to Lafayette, whom they regarded as too liberal. Lafayette, after conferring with Louis-Philippe (whom he admired personally), resigned as commander of the National Guard on December 27, 1830.

However, the marquis kept his seat in the Chamber of Deputies. For the next three years, he spoke out strongly against what he viewed as the increasingly reactionary policies of the Louis-Philippe regime. Lafayette also continued his ardent support for revolutionary movements outside France, including those in Poland, Belgium, and Italy.

❖

Lafayette's last speech in the Chamber of Deputies came on January 3, 1834—a typically passionate defense of republicanism. In February, Lafayette contracted pneumonia after attending a rainy outdoor funeral. The Marquis de Lafayette died at 4:00 A.M. on May 20, 1834, four months short of his seventy-seventh birthday.

Louis-Philippe, fearing antigovernment demonstrations, did not allow the marquis' family to have a public funeral. Instead, the king ordered that a military funeral take place, and Lafayette was buried alongside his wife in Picpus Cemetery in Paris. His son, Georges, sprinkled on the coffin the soil that the marquis brought back with him from America in 1825.

When word of Lafayette's death crossed the Atlantic, America went into mourning. Flags flew at half-mast; memorial services took place in hundreds of cities and towns. President Andrew Jackson ordered that the French marquis receive the same funeral honors President John Adams had ordered for George Washington in 1799. The U.S. House and Senate were draped in black bunting for the rest of the 1834 session, and all members of the two bodies wore badges of mourning for thirty days. A congressional resolution urged American citizens to wear a similar badge for the same period.

"The name of Lafayette shall stand enrolled upon the annals of our race," John Quincy Adams said during his three-hour eulogy in Congress later that year, "high on the list of the pure and disinterested benefactors of mankind."[14]

Conclusion

Lafayette valued reputation and glory, but cared little for the power that generally results from them.

—Jules Cloquet, 1836[1]

THE MARQUIS DE LAFAYETTE FIGURED PROMINENTLY AS A MILITARY MAN and high-level political figure in two of history's most significant events: the American and French Revolutions. He was also an instrumental player in the lesser-known but crucial French Revolution of July 1830. Although some historians and others have pointed out that his motives involved a quest for glory—a not uncommon trait in humans—it is beyond question that he risked his life on countless occasions for the lofty principles he cherished: republicanism and freedom.

On the field of battle, Lafayette's most notable accomplishments were masterminding and carrying out the Virginia Peninsula Campaign in the spring and summer of 1781, which led to the victory at Yorktown, and commanding the French National Guard. In the latter position, he tamped down the excesses of the French Revolution in Paris from just after the storming of the Bastille in

July 1789 until the fall of 1791. Those were the biggest but certainly not the only achievements of Lafayette's military and political career. He was fearless under fire and nearly always made exemplary tactical decisions when the lead was flying. More than any other individual, the marquis was also responsible for securing vital French financial and military support for the Continental Army during the American Revolution.

Then there was the critical and pivotal role Lafayette played during the July Revolution of 1830 in France. During those three hot summer days, Lafayette, more than anyone else in France, prevented things from devolving into chaos and anarchy. And he played arguably the leading role in overseeing an all-but peaceful regime change from the autocratic Charles X to the republican-leaning monarch Louis-Philippe.

Off the battlefield, Lafayette strutted—and to a lesser extent, fretted—upon the highest levels of the French and American political stages from the late 1770s to the early 1830s. He did so by working closely with an astounding number of the most important and influential American and French leaders of the age. That list of Lafayette's American close friends and colleagues includes Thomas Jefferson, Thomas Paine, George Washington, Benjamin Franklin, John Adams, James Madison, James Monroe, John Quincy Adams, Daniel Webster, Andrew Jackson, James Fenimore Cooper, and many others. The marquis' French friends and contemporaries include Germaine de Stael, Louis XVI, Marie Antoinette, Louis XVIII, Charles X, Louis-Philippe, Napoleon, Robespierre, and a slew of other prominent—if less-remembered—ministers, government officials, noblemen, clerics, and military men.

✦

What lessons can modern leaders learn from Lafayette's long, eventful life enmeshed in war, revolutions, and political upheaval? First, once the Marquis de Lafayette set his sights on a goal, he was unrelenting in doing everything in his power to attain it. That was true from the time Lafayette was a teenager until he was in his mid-seventies. Determined to go to America and fight the British, and then to lead a division of troops, Lafayette persistently pushed against great odds and succeeded. Later in life, he worked assiduously for what we now call human rights—including freedom of speech and freedom of religion—in his native country and in his adopted one, the United States. He labored diligently, using all of his resources, contacts, and persuasive powers. The latter included communicating effectively. An ardent letter writer, Lafayette often penned four or five letters a day.

Second, Lafayette learned early in life to adopt multifaceted strategies and to be flexible. At heart, he was an aggressive warrior from the moment he first set foot on a battlefield at age nineteen. But he soon learned that there is much more to fighting a war than being bold, assertive, and fearless when the bullets are flying.

Lafayette learned during the American Revolution that an army needs consistent logistical support or it cannot fight. He discovered that an army needs political support as well. And he found out how to make sure that all that logistical and political support was forthcoming. He carried out those lessons again during the French Revolution—at least for its first two years.

Third, Lafayette, even though he was a born-and-bred nobleman, learned the value of being in the trenches with his troops. He was nearly always upbeat and led by example. His zealousness and continued optimism worked; those who served under him invariably praised him as a great, inspiring leader. He proved to be a successful, on-the-ground general, as well—a man who never faltered in battle. Through victory and tactical retreats, Lafayette never was outthought or outfought on the field of battle. And, as we have seen, many believe that his guerrilla-like campaign on the Virginia Peninsula against Cornwallis proved to be the key to the ultimate victory in the Revolutionary War.

The Marquis de Lafayette was far from perfect. He was sometimes vain, naïve, immature, and egocentric. But he consistently stuck to his ideals, even when doing so endangered his life and fortune. Those ideals proved to be the founding principles of two of the world's most enduring nations, the United States and France. That is a legacy that few military leaders, politicians, or statesmen can match.

Notes

Introduction

1. Lafayette to Henry Laurens, president of the Continental Congress, September 23, 1778, in Marquis de Lafayette, *Memoirs, Correspondence and Manuscripts of General Lafayette Published by His Family* (New York: Saunders and Otley, 1837), Vol. I, 220. Also see Stanley J. Idzerda et al., eds., *Lafayette in the Age of the American Revolution: Selected Letters and Papers, 1776–1790* (Ithaca, N.Y.: Cornell University Press, 1979), Vol. II, 180.
2. President Franklin D. Roosevelt, Address to Congress, "On the One Hundredth Anniversary of the Death of Lafayette," May 20, 1934.
3. George Washington to Lafayette, May 18, 1778, in John C. Fitzpatrick, ed., *The Writings of George Washington from the Original Manuscript Sources, 1745–1799* (Washington D.C.: U.S. Government Printing Office, 1934), Vol. XI, 418.
4. Lafayette, *Memoirs,* Vol. I, 47.
5. Lafayette to Thomas Jefferson, April 21, 1781, Library of Virginia, *Lafayette: Letters, 1781–1825,* accession 24034.

Chapter 1

1. Marquis de Lafayette, *Memoirs, Correspondence and Manuscripts of General Lafayette* (New York: Saunders and Otley, 1837); quoted in Harlow Giles Unger, *Lafayette* (New York: Wiley, 2002), 7.

2. Many biographies of Lafayette have been written since his death in 1834. This account of his early years is based primarily on the relevant material in *Lafayette Comes to America* (Chicago: University of Chicago, 1935), the first volume of Louis R. Gottschalk's four-volume biography; Andre Maurois, *Adrienne: The Life of the Marquise de la Fayette* (London: Jonathan Cape, 1961), translated by Gerard Hopkins; Olivier Bernier, *Lafayette: Hero of Two Worlds* (New York: Dutton, 1983); Unger, *Lafayette;* David A. Clary, *Adopted Son: Washington, Lafayette, and the Friendship That Saved the Revolution* (New York: Bantam, 2007); and Stanley J. Idzerda's biographical essay in Stanley J. Idzerda, Anne C. Loveland, and Marc H. Miller, *Lafayette, Hero of Two Worlds: The Art and Pageantry of His Farewell Tour of America, 1824–1825* (Hanover, N.H., and London: University Press of New England/Queens Museum, 1989). The family name was sometimes spelled "La Fayette," but for more than two centuries the accepted spelling—even in France—has been "Lafayette."

3. Clary, 14.

4. Maurois, 36. Also see Clary, 10.

5. Etienne Charavay, *Le General La Fayette, 1757–1834, Notice Biographique* (Paris: Société de la Revolution Française, 1898), 4; also see Unger, 3.

6. Lafayette, *Memoirs,* quoted by Unger, 7.

7. Gottschalk, Vol. I, 18–20, and Clary, 15. King Clovis I (ca. 466–511) was the fifth-century Frankish king who defeated the Romans, Burgundians, and Visigoths; united the Franks; introduced Christianity; and thereby formed the basis for the nation of France.

8. John Quincy Adams, *Oration on the Life and Character of Gilbert Motier de Lafayette* (Washington D.C.: Gales and Seaton, 1835), 15.

9. Abigail Adams to Mrs. Cranch, December 9, 1784, in L. H. Butterfield, ed., *Adams Family Correspondence* (Cambridge, Mass.: Harvard University Press, 1963), Vol. VI, 15–16.

10. Stanley J. Idzerda et al., eds., *Lafayette in the Age of the American Revolution: Selected Letters and Papers, 1776–1790* (Ithaca, N.Y.: Cornell University Press, 1979), Vol. I, 3, 7.

11. Clary, 28. Freemasonry is a fraternal organization founded in the late sixteenth century. Its members subscribe to a set of moral and spiritual beliefs and engage in charitable activities—guided by these principles—which emphasize the belief in a supreme being. Freemasonry's symbols make widespread use of stonemasons' tools and implements.

12. Lafayette, *Memoirs,* Vol. I, 6.

13. Ibid., 7.

14. Ibid., 9.

15. Ibid., 8.

16. Ibid., 13. Also see Unger, 22.

17. Idzerda et al., eds., Vol. I, 7–8.

Chapter 2

1. Marquis de Lafayette, *Memoirs, Correspondence and Manuscripts of General Lafayette* (New York: Saunders and Otley, 1837), Vol. I, 9.
2. See Gerald M. Carbone, *Washington: Lessons in Leadership* (New York: Palgrave Macmillan, 2010), 104.
3. George Washington to Samuel Washington, December 18, 1776, in W. W. Abbott and Dorothy Twohig, eds., *The Papers of George Washington: Colonial Series* (Charlottesville: University of Virginia Press, 1977), Vol. VII, 370–371.
4. Lafayette, *Memoirs*, Vol. I, 9.
5. Ibid.
6. Louis R. Gottschalk, *Lafayette Comes to America* (Chicago: University of Chicago, 1935), Vol. I, 88.
7. Lafayette, *Memoirs*, Vol. I, 11.
8. Gottschalk, Vol. I, 90.
9. Idzerda et al., eds., Vol. I, 28.
10. Henri Doniol, *Histoire de la Participation de la France à l'Etablissement des Etats-unis d'Amérique* (Paris: Imprimerie Nationale, 1886), Vol. II, 395. Also see Harlow Giles Unger, *Lafayette* (New York: Wiley, 2002), 25.
11. Mme. De Lasteryie, *Vie de Madame de Lafayette par Mme. De Lasteryie* . . . (Paris: Léon Techener, 1868), 197–198. Also see Unger, 26.
12. Gottschalk, Vol. I, 104.
13. Doniol, Vol. II, 386. Also see Unger, 26.
14. Lafayette to Adrienne de Lafayette from aboard *La Victoire*, June 1777. Cleveland State University Library Special Collections, Marquis de Lafayette Collection, Christine Valadon, translator, Reel 23, Folder 202.
15. Ibid.
16. Ibid.
17. Ibid.
18. Ibid.
19. Lafayette, *Memoirs*, Vol. I, 14.
20. Lafayette to Adrienne de Lafayette, June 15, 1777, Cleveland State University Library Special Collections, Marquis de Lafayette Collection, Christine Valadon, translator, Reel 23, Folder 202.
21. Ibid. Also see Idzerda et al., eds., Vol. I, 60.

Chapter 3

1. John Quincy Adams, *Oration on the Life and Character of Gilbert Motier de Lafayette* (Washington D.C.: Gales and Seaton, 1835), 11.
2. Memoir by the Chevalier Dubuysson, in Stanley J. Idzerda et al., eds., *Lafayette in the Age of the American Revolution, Selected Letters and Papers*

(Ithaca, N.Y.: Cornell University Press, 1977), Vol. I, 75. Also see James S. Gaines, *For Liberty and Glory: Washington, Lafayette and Their Revolutions* (New York: Norton, 2007), 62–63.

3. Lafayette, *Memoirs,* Vol. I, 14.
4. Ibid, 15.
5. Journal of a Campaign in America by Du Russeau de Fayoll, in Idzerda et al., eds., Vol. I, 69, 71.
6. Louis R. Gottschalk, *Lafayette Comes to America* (Chicago: University of Chicago, 1935), 129.
7. Ibid.
8. Memoir by the Chevalier Dubuysson, in Idzerda et al., eds., Vol. I, 77.
9. Harlow Giles Unger, *Lafayette* (New York: Wiley, 2002), 37.
10. Marquis de Lafayette, *Memoirs, Correspondence and Manuscripts of General Lafayette* (New York: Saunders and Otley, 1837), Vol. I, 18.
11. Lafayette, *Memoirs,* translated in Idzerda et al., eds., Vol. I, 91.
12. Lafayette, *Memoirs,* Vol. I, 19.
13. Ibid, 23.
14. See Unger, 40; and David A. Clary, *Adopted Son: Washington, Lafayette, and the Friendship That Saved the Revolution* (New York: Bantam, 2007), 117 and note 468.
15. Lafayette to Adrienne de Lafayette, September 12, 1777, in Lafayette, *Memoirs,* Vol. I, 43. Also see Unger, 48.
16. Lafayette to George Washington, October 14, 1777, in Idzerda et al., eds., Vol. I, 122–123.
17. Unger, 49.
18. Washington to the president of Congress, November 1, 1777, in Idzerda et al., eds., Vol. I, 140.
19. Nathanael Greene to Washington, November 26, 1777, in Idzerda et al., eds., Vol. I, 158.
20. Washington to the president of Congress, November 26, 1777, in Idzerda et al., eds., Vol. I, 158.

Chapter 4

1. Lafayette to Adrienne de Lafayette from Valley Forge, January 6, 1778, Cleveland State University Library Special Collections, Marquis de Lafayette Collection, Reel 23, Folder 202.
2. George Washington to William Buchanan, February 7, 1778, *The George Washington Papers at the Library of Congress, 1741–1799,* Letterbook 5, 35.
3. Instructions for the Marquis de Lafayette, Major General in the Army of the United States, commanding an expedition into Canada, Department of State, Papers of the Old Congress, Vol. I, 18. Also see Harlow Giles Unger, *Lafayette*

(New York: Wiley, 2002), 64; and Stanley J. Idzerda et al., eds., *Lafayette in the Age of the American Revolution, Selected Letters and Papers* (Ithaca, N.Y.: Cornell University Press, 1977), Vol. I, 263–267.

4. Lafayette to Washington, February 9, 1778, in Idzerda et al., eds., Vol. I, 287.

5. Marquis de Lafayette, *Memoirs, Correspondence and Manuscripts of General Lafayette* (New York: Saunders and Otley, 1837), Vol. I, 39.

6. Ibid., 40.

7. Lafayette to Washington, February 19, 1778, in Idzerda et al., eds., Vol. I, 300.

8. Lafayette to the president of Congress, February 20, 1778, in Idzerda et al., eds., Vol. I, 306.

9. Lafayette to Washington, February 23, 1778, in Idzerda et al., eds., Vol. I, 322.

10. Lafayette to Henry Laurens, February 23, 1778, in Idzerda et al., eds., Vol. I, 319.

11. *Journals of the Continental Congress, 1774–1789,* Monday, March 2, 1778, 216–217.

12. Washington to Lafayette, March 20, 1778, in Idzerda et al., eds., Vol. I, 372.

13. Lafayette to Washington, March 25, 1778, in Idzerda et al., eds., Vol. I, 380.

14. Treaty of Alliance Between The United States and France; February 6, 1778, Article 8, Library of Congress, "U.S. Congressional Documents and Debates, 1774–1875, Statutes at Large," 6.

15. Washington to the president of Congress, May 1, 1778, in John C. Fitzpatrick, ed., *The Writings of George Washington from the Original Manuscript Sources, 1745–1799* (Washington D.C.: U.S. Government Printing Office, 1934), Vol. XI, 331.

16. General Orders, May 1, 1778, in Fitzpatrick, ed., Vol. XI, 353.

Chapter 5

1. Quoted in Edward G. Lengel, *General George Washington: A Military Life* (New York: Random House, 2005), 294. Also see James S. Gaines, *For Liberty and Glory: Washington, Lafayette and Their Revolutions* (New York: Norton, 2007), 114.

2. Marquis de Lafayette, *Memoirs, Correspondence and Manuscripts of General Lafayette* (New York: Saunders and Otley, 1837), Vol. I, 51.

3. Lafayette, *Memoirs,* translated in Stanley J. Idzerda et al., eds., *Lafayette in the Age of the American Revolution, Selected Letters and Papers* (Ithaca, N.Y.: Cornell University Press, 1977), Vol. II, 10.

4. Lafayette to George Washington, June 24, 1778, in Idzerda et al., eds., Vol. II, 86.

5. Washington to Lafayette, June 25, 1778, in Idzerda et al., eds., Vol. II, 86.
6. Lafayette, *Memoirs,* translated in Idzerda et al., eds., Vol. II, 10.
7. Charles Lee to Washington, June 25, 1778. *George Washington Papers at the Library of Congress, 1741–1799: Series 4. General Correspondence. 1697–1799,* 468.
8. Washington to Lafayette, June 26, 1778, in Idzerda et al., eds., Vol. II, 94.
9. John C. Fitzpatrick, ed., *The Writings of George Washington from the Original Manuscript Sources, 1745–1799* (Washington D.C.: U.S. Government Printing Office, 1934), Vol. XII, 144.
10. See Lafayette, *Memoirs,* translated in Idzerda et al., eds., Vol. II, 11.
11. Quoted in Lengel, 294. Also see Gaines, 114.
12. Fitzpatrick, ed., Vol. XII, 144.
13. Ibid., 202.
14. Charlemagne Tower Jr., *The Marquis de La Fayette in the American Revolution* (Philadelphia: Lippincott, 1895), Vol. I, 439. Also see Harlow Giles Unger, *Lafayette* (New York: Wiley, 2002), 81.
15. Lafayette to Washington, September 6, 1778, in Idzerda et al., eds., Vol. II, 133.
16. Lafayette, *Memoirs,* translated in Idzerda et al., eds., Vol. II, 14.
17. Ibid.
18. Ibid, 15.
19. Lafayette to Washington, September 1, 1778, in Idzerda et al., eds., Vol. II, 164.
20. Ibid, 163.
21. Ibid.
22. Lafayette to the president of Congress, September 23, 1778, in Idzerda et al., eds., Vol. II, 180.

Chapter 6

1. Lafayette to the Comte de Vergennes, June 10, 1779, in Henri Doniol, *Histoire de la Participation de la France à l'Etablissement des Estats-Unis d'Amérique* (Paris: Imprimerie Nationale, 1886), Vol. IV, 291. Also see Harlow Giles Unger, *Lafayette* (New York: Wiley, 2002), 101.
2. Lafayette to George Washington, September 7, 1778, in Marquis de Lafayette, *Memoirs, Correspondence and Manuscripts of General Lafayette* (New York: Saunders and Otley, 1837), Vol. I, 203.
3. Lafayette to the Comte d'Estaing, September 8, 1778, translated in Stanley J. Idzerda et al., eds., *Lafayette in the Age of the American Revolution, Selected Letters and Papers* (Ithaca, N.Y.: Cornell University Press, 1977), Vol. II, 169. In that letter, the barely twenty-one-year old Lafayette also said: "If I am a little

too enthusiastic (I confess that I always let myself be carried away), attribute it to my age."

4. Lafayette to the Duc d'Ayen, September 11, 1778, in Lafayette, *Memoirs,* Vol. I, 204–205.

5. Washington to Lafayette, September 25, 1778, in Idzerda et al., eds., Vol. II, 183.

6. John C. Fitzpatrick, ed., *The Writings of George Washington from the Original Manuscript Sources, 1745–1799* (Washington D.C.: U.S. Government Printing Office, 1934), Vol. XIII, 40.

7. Lafayette to the president of Congress, November 29, 1778, in Idzerda et al., eds., Vol. II, 205.

8. James Thacher, *Military Journal During the American Revolutionary War, from 1776 to 1783* (Boston: Cottons and Barnard, 1827), 153.

9. Ibid.

10. Lafayette said that "drinking Madeira wine effectually restored his health" in Boston. Lafayette, *Memoirs,* Vol. I, 65.

11. The President of Congress to Lafayette, January 3, 1779, in Idzerda et al., eds., Vol. II, 217.

12. Fitzpatrick, ed., Vol. XIII, 459.

13. Ibid.

14. Lafayette, *Memoirs,* Vol. I, 67.

15. Lafayette to Vergennes, June 10, 1779, in Doniol, Vol. IV, 291. Also see Unger, 101.

16. See André Corvisier and John Childs, *A Dictionary of Military History and the Art of War* (Oxford and Cambridge: Blackwell Publishers, 1994), 355.

17. Lafayette to Vergennes, July 18, 1779, in Idzerda et al., eds., Vol. II, 289.

18. Instructions from Vergennes, March 5, 1780, in Idzerda et al., eds., Vol. II, 364.

19. Ibid, 366.

Chapter 7

1. John Quincy Adams, *Oration on the Life and Character of Gilbert Motier de Lafayette* (Washington, D.C.: Gales and Seaton, 1835), 32.

2. Lafayette to George Washington, April 27, 1780, in Marquis de Lafayette, *Memoirs, Correspondence and Manuscripts of General Lafayette* (New York: Saunders and Otley, 1837), Vol. I, 318.

3. Washington to Lafayette, March 18, 1780, in John C. Fitzpatrick, ed., *The Writings of George Washington from the Original Manuscript Sources, 1745–1799* (Washington, D.C.: U.S. Government Printing Office, 1934), Vol. XVIII, 122.

4. Friederich Kapp, *The Life of John Kalb: Major-General in The Revolutionary Army* (Bedford, Mass.: Applewood Books, 2009), 183.

5. Ibid.

6. Lafayette, *Memoirs,* Vol. I, 251.

7. Italics in original letter. Lafayette to Samuel Adams, May 30, 1780, in Stanley J. Idzerda et al., eds., *Lafayette in the Age of the American Revolution, Selected Letters and Papers* (Ithaca, N.Y.: Cornell University Press, 1977), Vol. III, 42.

8. Lafayette to Joseph Reed, May 31, 1780, ibid., 44.

9. Washington to Joseph Reed, May 28, 1780, in Fitzpatrick, ed., Vol. XVIII, 434.

10. Washington to the Comte de Rochambeau, July 16, 1780, in Fitzpatrick, ed., Vol. XIX, 186.

11. Lafayette to Washington, July 21, 1780, in Idzerda et al., eds., Vol. III, 103.

12. Rochambeau to the Chevalier de La Luzerne, August 14, 1780, in Idzerda et al., eds., Vol. III, 141.

13. Washington to Lafayette, July 27, 1780, in Idzerda et al., eds., Vol. III, 112.

14. Lafayette to the Vicomte de Noailles, September 2, 1780, in Idzerda et al., eds., Vol. III, 156.

15. Louis R. Gottschalk, *Lafayette and the Close of the American Revolution* (Chicago: University of Chicago Press, 1942), 122. Also see James S. Gaines, *For Liberty and Glory: Washington, Lafayette and Their Revolutions* (New York: Norton, 2007), 141.

16. James Thacher, *Military Journal During the American Revolutionary War, from 1776 to 1783* (Boston: Cottons and Barnard, 1827), 153.

17. Lafayette to Noailles, October 28, 1780, in Idzerda et al., eds., Vol. III, 209.

18. Washington to Lafayette, October 30, 1780, in Idzerda et al., eds., Vol. III, 214.

19. Lafayette, *Memoirs,* Vol. I, 257.

Chapter 8

1. Lafayette to George Washington, May 24, 1781, in Stanley J. Idzerda et al., eds., *Lafayette in the Age of the American Revolution, Selected Letters and Papers* (Ithaca, N.Y.: Cornell University Press, 1977), Vol. IV, 124.

2. Instructions from George Washington, February 20, 1781, in Idzerda et al., eds., Vol. III, 335.

3. Lafayette to Jefferson, March 17, 1781, in Idzerda et al., eds., Vol. III, 402.

4. Jefferson to Lafayette, March 10, 1781, in Idzerda et al., eds., Vol. III, 390.

5. Lafayette to Washington, March 26, 1781, in Idzerda et al., eds., Vol. III, 417.

6. John C. Fitzpatrick, ed., *The Writings of George Washington from the Original Manuscript Sources, 1745–1799* (Washington D.C.: U.S. Government Printing Office, 1934), Vol. XI, 421.

7. Lafayette to Washington, April 8, 1781, in Marquis de Lafayette, *Memoirs, Correspondence and Manuscripts of General Lafayette* (New York: Saunders and Otley, 1837), Vol. I, 400.

8. Lafayette to Washington, April 10, 1781, in Idzerda et al., eds., Vol. IV, 19–24.

9. Washington to John Laurens, April 9, 1871, in Fitzpatrick, ed., Vol. XXI, 439.

10. Lafayette to the Chevalier de La Luzerne, April 10, 1781, in Fitzpatrick, ed., Vol. XXI, 453–454. Also see Harlow Giles Unger, *Lafayette* (New York: Wiley, 2002), 134.

11. Lafayette, *Memoirs*, Vol. I, 260.

12. Lafayette to Jefferson, April 21, 1781, Library of Virginia, *Lafayette, Letters, 1781–1825*, accession 24034.

13. Nathanael Greene to Lafayette, May 1, 1781, in Idzerda et al., eds., Vol. IV, 74.

14. Robert E. Lee, ed., *Henry Lee: Memoirs of the War in the Southern Department of the United States* (New York: University Publishing Company, 1869), 313.

15. Ibid.

16. Quoted in Charlemagne Tower Jr., *The Marquis de La Fayette in the American Revolution* (Philadelphia: Lippincott, 1895), Vol. II, 238. Also see Unger, 144; and Lafayette, *Memoirs*, Vol. I, 264.

17. Lafayette to Washington, May 24, 1781, in Lafayette, *Memoirs*, Vol. I, 417.

18. Lafayette to Noailles, May 22, 1781, in Idzerda et al., eds., Vol. IV, 124.

19. Lafayette to Greene, June 18, 1781, in Idzerda et al., eds., Vol. IV, 523.

20. Major Ebenezer Denny, *Military Journal* (Philadelphia: J. B. Lippincott & Company/Historical Society of Pennsylvania, 1859), 37.

21. Ibid.

22. Lafayette to Noailles, July 9, 1781, in Idzerda et al., eds., Vol. IV, 241.

23. William B. Willcox, ed., *The American Rebellion: Sir Henry Clinton's Narrative of His Campaigns, 1775–1782* (New Haven, Conn.: Yale University Press, 1954), 337.

24. Washington to Lafayette, August 18, 1781, in Fitzpatrick, ed., Vol. XXIII, 33.

Chapter 9

1. Major Ebenezer Denny, *Military Journal* (Philadelphia: J. B. Lippincott & Company/Historical Society of Pennsylvania, 1859), 39.

2. James Thacher, *Military Journal During the American Revolutionary War, from 1776 to 1783* (Boston: Cottons and Barnard, 1827), 262.

3. Lafayette to Thomas Nelson, August 30, 1781, in Stanley J. Idzerda et al., eds., *Lafayette in the Age of the American Revolution, Selected Letters and Papers* (Ithaca, N.Y.: Cornell University Press, 1977), Vol. IV, 368–369.

4. Marquis de Lafayette, *Memoirs, Correspondence and Manuscripts of General Lafayette* (New York: Saunders and Otley, 1837), Vol. I, 269.

5. Ibid.

6. William Feltman, *The Journal of Lieut. William Feltman of the First Pennsylvania Regiment, 1781–82* (Philadelphia: Historical Society of Pennsylvania, 1853), 12.

7. Lafayette to George Washington, September 8, 1781, in Idzerda et al., eds., Vol. IV, 393.

8. St. George Tucker, "The Southern Campaign, 1781, From Guilford Court House to the Siege of York, Narrated in the Letters from Judge St. George Tucker to his Wife," in Charles Washington Coleman Jr., ed., *The Magazine of American History with Notes and Queries,* VII (New York: Historical Publication Co., 1881), 212.

9. Feltman, 13.

10. Denny, 39.

11. Washington to the Comte de Grasse, September 25, 1781, in Jared Sparks, ed., *The Writings of George Washington* (Boston: Ferdinand Andrews, 1840), Vol. VIII, 164

12. Lafayette, *Memoirs,* Vol. I, 270.

13. Lafayette to Washington, September 30, 1781, in Idzerda et al., eds., Vol. IV, 412.

14. See Jerome A. Greene, *The Allies at Yorktown: A Bicentennial History of the Siege of 1781* (Denver: Historic Preservation Division, National Park Service, U.S. Dept. of the Interior 1976).

15. Jonathan Trumbull, "Minutes of Occurrences Respecting the Siege and Capture of York in Virginia, extracted from the Journal of Colonel Jonathan Trumbull, Secretary to the General, 1781," *Proceedings of the Massachusetts Historical Society,* IV (Boston: Massachusetts Historical Society, 1876), 335.

16. Lafayette to the Chevalier de La Luzerne, September 30, 1781, translated in Idzerda et al., eds., Vol. IV, 407.

17. Lafayette to La Luzerne, October 3, 1781, translated in Idzerda et al., eds., Vol. IV, 415.

18. Lafayette to La Luzerne, October 12, 1781, translated in Idzerda et al., eds., Vol. IV, 416.

19. Denny, 41.

20. Artillery statistics from Colonel H. L. Landers, *The Virginia Campaign and the Blockade and Siege of Yorktown, 1781* (Washington, D.C.: U.S. Government Printing Office, 1931), 192.

21. William B. Willcox, ed., *The American Rebellion: Sir Henry Clinton's Narrative of His Campaigns, 1775–1782* (New Haven, Conn.: Yale University Press, 1954), 581.

22. Denny, 41.

23. Thacher, 275.
24. Denny, 42.
25. Feltman, 20.
26. Thacher, 277.
27. Charles Ross, ed., *Correspondence of Charles, First Marquis, Cornwallis* (London: John Murray, 1859), Vol. I, 125.
28. Benjamin Franklin Stevens, ed., *The Campaigns in Virginia, 1781, An Exact Reprint of Six Rare Pamphlets on the Clinton-Cornwallis Controversy* (London: privately printed, 1888), Vol. II, 212.
29. Thacher, 278.
30. Robert E. Lee, ed., *Henry Lee: Memoirs of the War in the Southern Department of the United States* (New York: University Publishing Company, 1869), 512. The legend has arisen that the British band played "The World Turned Upside Down" during the surrender ceremony. No primary source evidence supports that claim.
31. Thacher, 279.
32. Lafayette to the Comte de Maurepas, October 20, 1781, translated in Idzerda et al., eds., Vol. IV, 422.

Chapter 10

1. The Marquis de Ségur to Lafayette, December 5, 1781, in Stanley J. Idzerda et al., eds., *Lafayette in the Age of the American Revolution, Selected Letters and Papers* (Ithaca, N.Y.: Cornell University Press, 1977), Vol. IV, 447.
2. *Resolutions of Congress,* November 23, 1781, in Idzerda et al., eds., Vol. IV, 440.
3. Ségur to Lafayette, December 5, 1781, in Idzerda et al., eds., Vol. IV, 447.
4. The Comte de Vergennes to Lafayette, December 1, 1781, translated in Idzerda et al., eds., Vol. IV, 445–446.
5. Lafayette to George Washington, October 24, 1782, in Idzerda et al., eds., Vol. V, 64–65.
6. Lafayette to the Comtesse de Tessé, January 1, 1783, in Idzerda et al., eds., Vol. V, 77.
7. Lafayette to Washington, February 5, 1783, in Idzerda et al., eds., Vol. V, 91–92.
8. Washington to Lafayette, April 5, 1783, in Idzerda et al., eds., Vol. V, 121.
9. See Diane Windham Shaw, "Lafayette and Slavery," *Lafayette Alumni News Magazine,* Winter 2007.
10. Henry Knox to Lafayette, June 16, 1783, in Idzerda et al., eds., Vol. V, 137.
11. James Madison to Thomas Jefferson, September 7, 1784, in Idzerda et al., eds., Vol. V, 241.
12. Louis Gottschalk, *Lafayette Between the American and the French Revolutions* (Chicago: University of Chicago Press, 1950), 86. Also see James S. Gaines,

For Liberty and Glory: Washington, Lafayette and Their Revolutions (New York: Norton, 2007), 197.

13. Also known as the Iroquois Confederacy, the Six Nations consisted of the Mohawk, Oneida, Onandaga, Cayuga, Seneca, and Tuscarora tribes.
14. Lafayette address to the Continental Congress, December 11, 1784.
15. Abigail Adams to Mrs. Cranch, December 9, 1784, in L. H. Butterfield, ed., *Adams Family Correspondence* (Cambridge, Mass: Harvard University Press, 1993), Vol. VI, 15–16.
16. Lafayette to Washington, May 11, 1785, in Idzerda et al., eds., Vol. V, 322.
17. See S. K. Padover, ed., *The Complete Jefferson* (New York: Duell, Sloan & Pearce, 1943), 447–448.

Chapter 11

1. The Chevalier de La Luzerne to George Washington, January 17, 1790, in Jared Sparks, ed., *The Writings of George Washington: Being His Correspondence, Addresses, Messages and Other Papers, Official and Private* (Boston: Russel, Shattuck, and Williams, 1836), Vol. X, 88.
2. Horatio Gates to Benjamin Franklin, August 16, 1784, in *Benjamin Franklin Papers, 1731–1791* (Philadelphia: American Philosophical Society Library), Vol. XXXII, 83. Also see Stanley J. Idzerda et al., eds., *Lafayette in the Age of the American Revolution, Selected Letters and Papers* (Ithaca, N.Y.: Cornell University Press, 1977), Vol. V, xxv.
3. Lafayette to John Adams, April 9, 1787, in Louis Gottschalk and Shirley A. Bill, eds., *The Letters of Lafayette to Washington, 1777–1799* (Philadelphia: The American Philosophical Society, 1976), 338.
4. Brand Whitlock, *La Fayette* (New York: D. Appleton, 1929), Vol. I, 311. Also see Harlow Giles Unger, *Lafayette* (New York: Wiley, 2002), 223.
5. Thomas Paine to Washington, May 1, 1790, in Sparks, ed., Vol. IV, 328.
6. Thomas Carlyle, *The French Revolution: A History* (London: George Bell and Sons, 1902), Vol. I, 334.
7. Lafayette to Washington, January 12, 1790, in Gottschalk and Bill, eds., 346.
8. La Luzerne to George Washington, January 17, 1790, in Sparks, ed., Vol. IV, 310–311.
9. "Grand French Confederacy on Thursday, the Fourteenth of July 1790," *Times* of London, July 21, 1790. Also see Neil Fraistat and Susan S. Lanser, eds., *Maria Helen Williams, Letters Written in France: In the Summer 1790, to a Friend in England Containing Various Anecdotes Relative to the French Revolution* (Ontario: Broadview Press, 2001), 253.
10. Fraistat and Lanser, eds., 69.
11. Lafayette to Washington, August 23, 1790, in Gottschalk and Bill, eds., 349.
12. Ibid., 349–350.

13. Oscar Browning, ed., *The Dispatches Of Earl Gower, English Ambassador at Paris from June, 1790 To August, 1792* (1885) (Whitefish, Mont.: Kessinger Publishing, 2008), 98.

14. Quoted in, for example, Antonia Fraser, *Marie Antoinette: The Journey* (New York: Anchor, 2001), 345.

Chapter 12

1. Lafayette to George Washington, January 22, 1792, in Louis Gottschalk and Shirley A. Bill, eds., *The Letters of Lafayette to Washington, 1777–1799* (Philadelphia: The American Philosophical Society, 1976), 360.

2. *Les Révolutions de Paris,* no. 106, July 23–26, 1791.

3. Lafayette to William Short, November 16, 1791, quoted in Louis R. Gottschalk, *Lafayette and the Close of the American Revolution* (Chicago: University of Chicago Press, 1942), 421. Also see David A. Clary, *Adopted Son: Washington, Lafayette, and the Friendship That Saved the Revolution* (New York: Bantam, 2007), 402.

4. Gouverneur Morris to Washington, October 22, 1791, in Jared Sparks, ed., *Correspondence of the American Revolution: Being Letters of Eminent Men to George Washington, from the Time of His Taking Command of the Army to the End of His Presidency* (Boston: Little, Brown, and Company, 1853), Vol. IV, 409–411.

5. Lafayette to Washington, January 22, 1792, in Gottschalk and Bill, eds., 358–359.

6. General Rochambeau and Nicolas Luckner were subsequently imprisoned by the radicals. Rochambeau was released; Luckner was guillotined in Paris in 1794.

7. Morris to Washington, December 27, 1781, in Beatrix Carey Davenport, ed., *A Diary of the French Revolution by Gouverneur Morris (1752–1816), Minister to France During the Terror* (Boston: Houghton Mifflin, 1939), Vol. II, 334. Also see Harlow Giles Unger, *Lafayette* (New York: Wiley, 2002), 280.

8. Lafayette to Washington, January 22, 1792, in Gottschalk and Bill, eds., 360.

9. The Comte de Lally to Lord Sheffield, May 25, 1792, in "Unpublished Letters of the Comte de Lally in *The New Review:* Scenes from the French Revolution," in *Littell's Living Age* magazine, October 22, 1892, Vol. 195, 220.

10. Washington to Lafayette, June 10, 1792, in John C. Fitzpatrick, ed., *The Writings of George Washington from the Original Manuscript Sources, 1745–1799* (Washington D.C.: U.S. Government Printing Office, 1934), Vol. XXXII, 53.

11. Thomas Jefferson to Lafayette, June 16, 1792, in Paul Leicester Ford, ed., *The Writings of Thomas Jefferson, Vol. VI, 1792–1794* (New York: Putnam, 1895), 78.

12. Adolphe Thiers, trans. J. Dixon, *History of the French Revolution* (London: G. Vickers, 1845), Vol. I, 99.

13. Simon Schama called that episode "the beginning of the end of the reign of Louis XVI" in his book *Citizens: A Chronicle of the French Revolution* (New York: Knopf, 1989), 606.

14. Lally to Sheffield, June 21, 1792, in "Unpublished Letters," 222.

15. Quoted in Robert Asprey, *The Rise of Napoleon* (New York: Basic Books, 2000), 61.

16. Morris to Jefferson, August 1, 1792, in Davenport, ed., Vol. II, 483. Also see Anne Cary Morris, ed., *Diary and Letters of Gouverneur Morris: Minister of the United States to France; Member of the Constitutional Convention, etc.* (New York: Charles Scribner's Sons, 188), Vol. I, 566.

17. Lafayette to Adrienne de Lafayette, August 21, 1792, in Brand Whitlock, *La Fayette* (New York: D. Appleton, 1929), Vol. II, 58–59.

18. Lafayette to Short, August 26, 1792, in Etienne Charavay, *Le General La Fayette, 1757–1834, Notice Biographique* (Paris: Société de la Revolution Française, 1898), 582. Also see Unger, 287.

Chapter 13

1. Marquis de Lafayette, *Memoirs, Correspondence and Manuscripts of General Lafayette* (New York: Saunders and Otley, 1837), Vol. V, 174. Also see Stanley J. Idzerda, "Lafayette, Apostle of Liberty," in Stanley J. Idzerda, Anne C. Loveland, and Marc H. Miller, *Lafayette, Hero of Two Worlds: The Art and Pageantry of His Farewell Tour of America, 1824–1825* (Hanover, N.H., and London: University Press of New England/Queens Museum, 1989), 46.

2. "France," *London Times*, Monday, Sept. 10, 1792, p. 1.

3. William Short to Gouverneur Morris, November 12, 1792, and December 7, 1792, in Beatrix Carey Davenport, ed., *A Diary of the French Revolution by Gouverneur Morris (1752–1816), Minister to France During the Terror* (Boston: Houghton Mifflin, 1939), Vol. II, 556, 560. Also see Harlow Giles Unger, *Lafayette* (New York: Wiley, 2002), 291.

4. See Unger, 308. Connecticut was one of the states that had granted Lafayette and his family honorary citizenship during his 1784 visit.

5. Lafayette to George Washington, October 6, 1797, in Louis Gottschalk and Shirley A. Bill, eds., *The Letters of Lafayette to Washington, 1777–1799* (Philadelphia: The American Philosophical Society, 1976), 364.

6. Lafayette, *Memoirs*, Vol. V, 174. Also see Idzerda, "Lafayette, Apostle of Liberty," 46.

7. Brand Whitlock, *La Fayette* (New York: D. Appleton, 1929), Vol. II, 150.

8. Auguste Levasseur, trans. John D. Goodman, *Lafayette in America in 1824 and 1825: Journal of a Voyage to the United States* (Philadelphia: Carey and Lea, 1829), 13–14.

9. The first time a foreign dignitary addressed a joint session of Congress was May 20, 1934, when the French ambassador to the United States, André de Laboulaye, gave a speech marking the centennial of Lafayette's death.

10. *Central Gazette,* Charlottesville, Va., November 10, 1824.

11. Rep. Charles Fenton Mercer of Virginia, speaking on the U.S. House of Representatives floor on December 22, 1824, *Register of Debates, 18th Congress, 2nd Session,* 53.

Chapter 14

1. Russell M. Jones, "The Flowering of a Legend: Lafayette and the Americans," *French Historical Studies,* IV (1966), 401.

2. Ibid., 56.

3. Odilon Barrot, *Mémoirs Posthumes* (Paris: G. Charpentier, 1875), Vol. I, 112. Also see Lloyd Kramer, *Lafayette in Two Worlds: Public Cultures & Personal Identities in the Age of Revolutions* (Chapel Hill: University of North Carolina Press, 1996), 228.

4. Jules Cloquet, *Recollections of the Private Life of General Lafayette* (Boston: Leavitt, Lord & Co., 1836), Vol. I, 19–20.

5. Proclamation of the Deputies, July 31, 1830, in Frank Maloy Anderson, *The Constitutions and Other Select Documents Illustrative of the History of France, 1789–1901* (Minneapolis: H. W. Wilson Co., 1904), 502–503.

6. Brand Whitlock, *La Fayette* (New York: D. Appleton, 1929), Vol. II, 355. Also see Harlow Giles Unger, *Lafayette* (New York: Wiley, 2002), 367.

7. "Long live freedom."

8. Bernard Sarrans, *Memoirs of General Lafayette and of the French Revolution of 1830* (Boston: Lilly, Wait, Colman, and Holden, 1833), Vol. I, 236–237.

9. "Memoirs of Odilon-Barrot" in *London Quarterly Review* (Vol. CCLXXXVIII, October 1877), 173.

10. Sarrans, 237.

11. Ibid, 238.

12. Ibid., 166.

13. Jones, 401.

14. John Quincy Adams, *Oration on the Life and Character of Gilbert Motier de Lafayette* (Washington D.C.: Gales and Seaton, 1835), 88.

Conclusion

1. Jules Cloquet, *Recollections of the Private Life of General Lafayette* (Boston: Leavitt, Lord & Co., 1836), Vol. I, 24.

Bibliography

Abbott, W. W. and Dorothy Twohig, eds. *The Papers of George Washington: Colonial Series, Vols. 1–10*. Charlottesville: University of Virginia Press, 1983–1995.

Adams, John Quincy. *Oration on the Life and Character of Gilbert Motier de Lafayette*. Boston: S. Colman, and Russell, Odiorne & Co., 1835.

———. *Life of General Lafayette*. New York: Cornish, Lamport & Co., 1851.

Alden, John Richard. *George Washington: A Biography*. Baton Rouge: Louisiana State University Press, 1984.

Anderson, Troyer. *The Command of the Howe Brothers during the American Revolution*. New York and London: Oxford University Press, 1936.

Axelrod, Alan. *America's Wars*. New York: John Wiley & Sons, 2002.

Barclay, Sidney, ed. *Grace Barclay's Diary: Personal Recollections of the American Revolution*. New York: Anson D. F. Randolph, 1859.

Bemis, Samuel Flag. *The Diplomacy of the American Revolution*. Bloomington, Indiana: Indiana University Press, 1937.

Bernier, Olivier. *Lafayette: Hero of Two Worlds*. New York: E. P. Dutton, 1883.

Brandon, Edgar Ewing, ed. *Lafayette, Guest of the Nation: A Contemporary Account of the Triumphal Tour of General Lafayette through the United States in 1824–1825, as Reported by the Local Newspapers*. 3 vols. Oxford, Ohio: Oxford Historical Press 1950–1957.

Browning, Oscar, ed. *The Dispatches of Earl Gower, English Ambassador at Paris from June, 1790 to August, 1792 (1885)*. Whitefish, Montana: Kessinger Publishing, 2008.

Buckman, Peter. *Lafayette: A Biography*. New York: Paddington Press, 1977.

Carbone, Gerald M. *Washington: Lessons in Leadership*. New York: Palgrave Macmillan, 2010.

Chambers, John Whiteclay II, et al., eds. *The Oxford Companion to American Military History*. Oxford and New York: Oxford University Press, 1999.

Chastellux, François Jean. *Travels in North America in the Years 1780, 1781, 1782.* Bedford, Mass.: Applewood Books, 2009.

Chernow, Ron. *Alexander Hamilton.* New York: Penguin Books, 2005.

Chinard Gilbert, ed. *The Letters of Lafayette and Jefferson.* Baltimore: Johns Hopkins University Press, 1929.

Clary, David A. *Adopted Son: Washington, Lafayette, and the Friendship that Saved the Revolution.* New York: Bantam, 2007.

Cloquet, Jules. *Recollections of the Private Life of General Lafayette, Vol. I.* Boston: Leavitt, Lord & Co., 1836.

Collingham. H. A. C. *The July Monarchy: A Political History of France, 1830–1848.* London and New York: Longman, 1988.

Commanger, Henry Steele and Richard B. Morris. *Spirit of Seventy-Six: The Story of the American Revolution as Told by Participants.* New York: Da Capo, 1995.

Corwin, Edward S. Corwin. *French Policy and the American Alliance of 1778.* Princeton: Princeton University Press, 1916.

Denny, Major Ebenezer. *Military Journal of Major Ebenezer Denny, an Officer in the Revolutionary and Indian Wars.* Philadelphia: J. B. Lippincott & Co./Historical Society of Pennsylvania, 1859.

Doniol, Henri. *Histoire de la Participation de la France à l'Etablissement des Estats-Unis d'Amérique.* Paris: Imprimerie Nationale, 1886.

Doyle, William. *The Oxford History of the French Revolution.* Oxford and New York: Oxford University Press, 2003.

Ellis, Joseph J. *His Excellency: George Washington.* New York: Vintage Books, 2005.

Feltman, William. *The Journal of Lieut. William Feltman of the First Pennsylvania Regiment, 1781–82.* Philadelphia: The Historical Society of Pennsylvania, 1853.

Ferling, John E. *Almost a Miracle: Tthe American Victory in the War of Independence.* New York: Oxford University Press, 2007.

Fitzpatrick, John C., ed. *The Writings of George Washington from the Original Manuscript Sources, 1745–1799,* 39 vols. Washington, D.C.: U.S. Government Printing Office, 1931–1944.

Fraistat, Neil and Susan S. Lanser, eds. *Maria Helen Williams: Letters Written in France in the Summer 1790, to a Friend in England Containing Various Anecdotes Relative to the French Revolution.* Ontario: Broadview Press, 2001.

Fraser, Antonia. *Marie Antoinette: The Journey.* New York: Anchor Books, 2001.

Fredriksen, John C. *Revolutionary War Almanac: Facts on File Library of American History.* New York: Facts on File, 2006.

Furet, François, and Mona Ozouf, eds. *A Critical Dictionary of the French Revolution.* Cambridge: Harvard University Press, 1989.

Gaines, James R. *For Liberty and Glory: Washington, Lafayette, and Their Revolution.* New York: W. W. Norton, 2007.

Gerson, Noel B. *Statue in Search of a Pedestal: A Biography of the Marquis de La Fayette.* New York: Dodd, Mead, 1977.

Gottschalk, Louis R. *Lafayette Comes to America*. Chicago: University of Chicago Press, 1935.

——. *Lafayette Joins the American Army*. University of Chicago Press, 1937.

——. *Lady-in-Waiting: The Romance of Lafayette and Aglae de Hunolstine*. Baltimore: Johns Hopkins University Press, 1939.

——. *Lafayette and the Close of the American Revolution*. Chicago: University of Chicago Press, 1942.

——. *Lafayette between the American and the French Revolutions*. Chicago: University of Chicago Press, 1950.

——. *Lafayette in America, 1777–1783*. Arveyres, France: L'Esprit de Lafayette Society, 1975.

Gottschalk, Louis R. and Margaret Maddox. *Lafayette in the French Revolution*. Chicago: University of Chicago Press, 1969.

Gottschalk, Louis and Shirley A. Bill, eds. *The Letters of Lafayette to Washington, 1777–1799*. Philadelphia: The American Philosophical Society, 1976.

Guilhou, Marguerite. *Life of Adrienne d'Ayen, Marquise de Lafayette*. Translated by S. Richard Fuller. Chicago: Ralph Fletcher Seymour, 1918.

Hibbert, Christopher. *The Days of the French Revolution*. New York: Harper Perrennial, 1999.

Hoffman, Ronald and Peter J. Albert, eds. *Diplomacy and Revolution: The Franco-American Alliance of 1778*. Charlottesville: University Press of Virginia, 1981.

Holmes, Richard, ed. *The Oxford Companion to Military History*. Oxford and New York: Oxford University Press, 2001.

Idzerda, Stanley J. et al., eds. *Lafayette and the Age of the American Revolution: Selected Letters and Papers, 1776–1790*. 5 Vols. Ithaca, New York: Cornell University Press, 1977–1983.

——. *Lafayette, Hero of Two Worlds: The Art and Pageantry of His Farewell Tour of America, 1824–1825*. Hanover, N.H., and London: University Press of New England/The Queen's Museum, 1989.

James, Coy Hilton. *Silas Deane, Patriot or Traitor?* East Lansing: Michigan State University Press, 1975.

Johnston, Henry P. *The Yorktown Campaign and the Surrender of Cornwallis, 1781*. New York: Harper & Brothers, 1881.

Kapp, Friederich. *The Life of John Kalb: Major-General in the Revolutionary Army*. Bedford, Mass.: Applewood Books, 2009.

Kennett, Lee. *The French Forces in America, 1780–1783*. Westport, Conn.: Greenwood, 1977.

Ketchum, Richard M. *Victory at Yorktown: The Campaign That Won the Revolution*. New York: Henry Holt & Co., 2004.

Klamkin, Marian. *Return of Lafayette*. New York: Scribner, 1975.

Kramer, Lloyd. *Lafayette in Two Worlds: Public Cultures & Personal Identities in the Age of Revolutions*. Chapel Hill: University of North Carolina Press, 1996.

Kwasny, Mark V. *Washington's Partisan War, 1775–1783*. Kent, Ohio: Kent State University Press, 1998.

Lafayette, Marquis de. *Memoirs, Correspondence and Manuscripts of General Lafayette Published by His Family.* Vol. 1. New York: Saunders and Otley, 1837.

La Fuye, Maurice de, and Emile A. Babeau. *Apostle of Liberty: A Life of La Fayette.* New York: T. Yoseloff, 1956.

Latzko, Andreas. *Lafayette, A Life.* Translated by E. W. Dickes. New York: Doubleday, Doran & Co., 1936

Leckie, Robert. *The Wars of America.* New York: HarperCollins, 1992.

Lee, Robert E., ed., and Henry Lee. *Memoirs of the War in the Southern Department of the United States.* New York: University Publishing Company, 1869.

Lengel, Edward G. *General George Washington.* New York: Random House, 2005.

Levasseur, Auguste. *Lafayette in America in 1824 and 1825, or a Journal of a Voyage to the United States.* Translated by John D. Goodman. Philadelphia: Carey and Lea, 1829.

Lever, Evelyne and Catherine Temerson. *Marie Antoinette: The Last Queen of France.* New York: Farrar, Straus and Giroux, 2000.

Loth, David. *The People's General: Personal Story of Lafayette.* New York: Charles Scribner's Sons, 1951.

Mahan, A. T. *The Major Operations of the Navies in the War of American Independence.* London: Sampson Low, Marston & Co., 1913.

Mansel, Philip. *Paris Between Empires.* New York: St. Martin's Press, 2001.

Massey, Gregory. D. *John Laurens and the American Revolution.* Columbia: University of South Carolina Press, 2000.

Matloff, Maurice, ed., *American Military History: Volume I: 1775–1902.* Conshohocken, Pa.: Combined Books, 1996.

Maurois, Andre. *Adrienne: The Life of the Marquise de la Fayette.* Translated by Gerard Hopkins. London: Jonathan Cape, 1961.

McCarthy, Justin H. *The French Revolution.* New York: Harper and Brothers, 1898.

Miller, Melanie Randolph. *Envoy to the Terror: Gouverneur Morris and the French Revolution.* Dulles, Virginia: Potomac Books, 2005.

Morgan, George. *The True Lafayette.* Philadelphia: Lippincott, 1919.

Neely, Sylvia. *Lafayette and the Liberal Ideal, 1814–1824: Politics and Conspiracy in an Age of Reaction.* Carbondale, Ill.: Southern Illinois University Press, 1991.

Penman, John Simpson. *Lafayette and Three Revolutions.* Boston: Stratford & Co., 1929.

Perkins, James Breck. *France in the American Revolution.* Boston and New York: Houghton Mifflin, 1911.

Perret, Geoffrey. *A Country Made by War: From the Revolution to Vietnam—The Story of America's Rise to Power.* New York: Random House, 1989.

Pilbeam, Pamela. *The 1830 Revolution in France.* New York: Palgrave Macmillan, 1991.

Pinkney, David H. *French Revolution of 1830.* Princeton: Princeton University Press, 1972.

Purcell, Sarah J. *Sealed with Blood: War, Sacrifice, and Memory in Revolutionary America.* Philadelphia: University of Pennsylvania Press, 2002.

Ramsay, David. *The History of the American Revolution: In Two Volumes.* London: Johnson & Stockdale, 1791.

Randolph, Thomas Jefferson, ed. *Memoir, Correspondence, and Miscellanies from the Papers of Thomas Jefferson.* 4 Vols. Boston: Gray and Bowen, 1830.

Rees, James C. with Stephen Spignesi. *George Washington's Leadership Lessons.* New York: Wiley, 2007.

Royot, Daniel, ed. *La France et L'esprit de 76: Colloque du Bicentenaire de l'Indépendence des Etas-Unis.* Clermont-Ferrand, France: Association pour les Publications de la Faculté des Lettres et Sciences Humaines de Clermont-Ferrand, 1977.

Sarrans, Bernard. *Memoirs of General Lafayette and of the French Revolution of 1830.* Vol. I. Boston: Lilly, Wait, Colman, and Holden, 1833.

Schama, Simon. *Citizens: A Chronicle of the French Revolution.* New York: Knopf, 1991.

Scribner, Frank Kimball. *A Continental Cavalier: The Record of Some Incidents Pertaining to the Chevalier de Marc, Brevet Major in the Army of the Colonies, aid-de-camp to General, the Marquis Lafayette.* New York: Abbey Press, 1899.

Sedgwick, Henry D. *La Fayette.* Indianapolis: Bobbs-Merrill, 1928.

Smyth, Albert Henry, ed. *The Writings of Benjamin Franklin, Volume VIII, 1780–1782.* London: Macmillan, 1907.

Sparks, Jared, ed. *Correspondence of the American Revolution; Being Letters of Eminent Men to George Washington, from the Time of His Taking Command of the Army to the End of His Presidency,* Boston: Little, Brown, and Company, 1853.

Stewart, Richard W. *American Military History, Volume I: The United States Army and the Forging of a Nation, 1775–1917.* Washington, D.C.: U.S Army Center of Military History, Army Historical Series, 2005.

Thacher, James. *Military Journal During the American Revolutionary War, from 1776 to 1783.* 2nd ed. Boston: Cottons and Barnard, 1827.

Tower, Charlemagne Jr. *The Marquis de La Fayette in the American Revolution.* Philadelphia: Lippincott, 1895.

Tuchman, Barbara. *The First Salute.* New York: Ballantine, 1988.

Unger, Harlow Giles. *Lafayette.* New York: Wiley, 2002.

Whitlock, Brand. *La Fayette.* New York: D. Appleton, 1929.

Whitman, Walt. *Lafayette in Brooklyn.* New York: George D. Smith, 1905.

Willcox, William B. ed., *The American Rebellion: Sir Henry Clinton's Narrative of His Campaigns, 1775–1782.* New Haven: Yale University Press, 1954.

Woodward. W. E. *Lafayette.* New York: Farrar & Rinehart, Inc., 1938.

Wright, Constance. *Madame de Lafayette: The Story of a Patriot's Wife.* New York: Holt, Rinehart and Winston, 1959.

Zucker, A. E. *General De Kalb, Lafayette's Mentor.* Chapel Hill: University of North Carolina Press, 1966.

Index

Lafayette's early career and actions in America are indexed under Lafayette, Gilbert. Actions following his return to France in 1782 and during the French Revolution are indexed under Lafayette, Marquis de. Lesser-known British and American figures are identified with the suffix (Br), (CA), and (AP). Designations stand for (British), (Continental Army), and (American politician), respectively.